# Better than peanut
## butter & jelly

# Better than peanut butter & jelly

Quick Vegetarian Meals Your Kids Will Love!
Revised Edition

**Marty Mattare & Wendy Muldawer**

McBooks Press, Inc.
Ithaca, New York

Published by McBooks Press 2006
Copyright © 2006 Marty Mattare & Wendy Muldawer

Cover and text designed by Panda Musgrove
Cover Photo: Alamy Images

ISBN: 978-1-59013-122-0
      1-59013-122-3


Library of Congress Cataloging-in-Publication Data

Mattare, Marty, 1944–
Better than peanut butter and jelly : quick vegetarian meals your kids will love!/ by Marty Mattare & Wendy Muldawer.—Rev. ed.
     p. cm.
  Rev. ed. of: Quick vegetarian meals your kids will love! / by Wendy Muldawer and Marty Mattare. c1998.
  ISBN-13: 978-1-59013-122-0 (trade pbk. : alk. paper)
  ISBN-10: 1-59013-122-3
I. Muldawer, Wendy, 1962– II. Muldawer, Wendy, 1962– Quick vegetarian meals your kids will love! III. Title.
  TX837.M84 2006
  641.5'636—dc22
                        2005024885


Distributed to the trade by National Book Network, Inc.
15200 NBN Way, Blue Ridge Summit, PA 17214
800-462-6420


Additional copies of this book may be ordered from any bookstore or directly from McBooks Press, Inc., ID Booth Building, 520 North Meadow St., Ithaca, NY 14850. Please include $5.00 postage and handling with mail orders. New York State residents must add sales tax to total remittance (books & shipping). All McBooks Press publications can also be ordered by calling toll-free 1-888-BOOKS11 (1-888-266-5711).

Please call to request a free catalog.
Visit the McBooks Press website at www.mcbooks.com.

Printed in the United States of America
9 8 7 6 5 4 3 2 1

# table of Contents

# Acknowledgements:

We want to thank the children who contributed their art work for this edition of our book. Their whimsical drawings illustrate why we wrote *Better Than Peanut Butter & Jelly* in the first place. We believe in wholesome, healthy food for happy, healthy children.

The artists:

Brooke Brecht
Joey Bromley
Michael Bromley
Jenna Federation
Tess Federation
Nikiah Hakes
Taiya Hakes
Mason Hill
Camille Holmes
Emilie Holmes
Noah Kinne
Jacob Klumpp
Logan Klumpp
Sean Muldawer
Beyla Munach
Tempe Munach
Lindzey Nicholson
Isabella Pearl Romeo-Hall
Ethan Skutt

"Children who acquire a taste for chicken nuggets, roast beef and French fries today are the cancer patients and weight-loss clinic patients of tomorrow."

**Neal Barnard, MD**

*Food for Life*

"For more than thirty-two years, I've been encouraging parents to reduce or eliminate their children's meat consumption. Children who don't eat meat will be, in my opinion, among those adults in the next generation with no heart disease and cancer."

**Charles R. Attwood, MD**

*Dr. Attwood's
Low-Fat Prescription for Kids*

# About this book

*Better Than Peanut Butter & Jelly* is a cookbook for busy parents who are concerned about good nutrition for their children. It features more than 150 healthy, meatless meals and snacks for children age two and up. The recipes contain no refined sugar and are low in fat. All are high in nutrients, including protein and essential vitamins and minerals. They also rate high in the flavors, colors, and textures kids seem to prefer. To make the recipes even more child-friendly, we've limited the use of spices and strongly flavored ingredients. (If your children happen to like spicy food, feel free to experiment by adding more garlic, a bit of hot pepper, or other spices to taste.)

Although this is a vegetarian cookbook, you don't have to be a vegetarian to use it. Many people these days are "semi-vegetarians." They have added many more vegetarian meals to their diets but still occasionally eat meat, fish, or poultry. Please add this book to your cookbook shelf and refer to it on those days and nights when you want to serve healthy, vegetarian food to your family.

Lacto-ovo vegetarians—who consume milk and eggs but not meat, fish, or poultry—will find this book very appropriate. And vegans—who consume no animal products at all—fare very well, too. Almost half of the recipes in this book are actually vegan.

The vegan diet is growing in the United States. There are many reasons for this growth, among them, concern for the environment as well as for health. Nutritionists support a vegan diet for children as long as the diet is carefully monitored for the proper amount of nutrients. Research finds that the vegan child, by age ten, is in the same percentile for height but 10 percent lower in weight than the omnivorous child who eats meat as well as plant-based food. Parents need to pay particular attention to calories, protein, calcium, iron, zinc, vitamin B12, and vitamin D. There is data available about how much of each of these is necessary for good health, so it is not difficult to raise a child as a vegan.

We have included in the book a list of items for the "well-stocked pantry" and the "well-stocked refrigerator." If you keep even a few of these food items in your home, you'll be able to create fast and nutritious meals at any time. At the end of the book, you'll find a chart of important nutritional elements found in most of the ingredients we use in our recipes. The chart lists the amount of calories, protein, fat, and carbohydrates in many foods. Following that is a list of resources for vegetarians that includes some mail-order companies in case you can't find certain items on the shelves in your local grocery store. Today, most grocery chains carry at least some meatless products, and some carry a significant number of products.

For those of you who want to start your children on the path to vegetarianism or to more healthful eating in general, this book will help you introduce interesting and tasty alternatives to meat and animal products, and also help your children acquire a taste for vegetables, whole-grains, and generally wholesome foods. For those who are already vegetarians or vegans and are raising your children as such, we hope this book will provide you the means to serve a variety of interesting meals that your entire family will enjoy!

## Why We Wrote Our Own Cookbook

As mothers and vegetarians, we had many reasons for wanting to write *Better Than Peanut Butter & Jelly.*

### From Wendy's point of view

As a mother who raised an elementary-school-aged boy as a vegetarian, I found myself one day packing the second peanut butter-and-jelly sandwich of the week for his school lunch, and I thought to myself, "There must be other things I can make for Sean's lunches that are meatless, healthy, and easy—but will taste good, too."

I combed through my collection of vegetarian cookbooks but knew I'd have a hard time convincing my then six year old to try any of the spicy or sophisticated recipes I found. These books, wonderful as they are, are written for adult tastes and adult expectations of vegetarian cuisine. Then I bought the only two cookbooks I could find that featured "kid food" with hopes that I'd be able to use the meatless recipes they contained. To my dismay, the few non-meat recipes in these books concentrated heavily on whole milk, cheese, vegetable oil, butter, sour cream, and sugar: not exactly my idea of healthy! I wanted something better, and it occurred to me that many moms, vegetarian or not, needed the same kind of help I did. Now, some years later, even though today you can find more vegetarian cookbooks to buy, there are still very few that focus on children!

**From Marty's point of view**

I wish I had known the health benefits of a low-fat, vegetarian diet when I was raising my two children in the late '60s. Back then, the standard "kid" fare was fast-food hamburgers and French fries on Saturday; meat loaf on Sunday; hot dogs on Monday; fried chicken on Tuesday (you get the point); and bowls of ice cream every day. Actually, that "standard" fare seems standard even today. And, now worse than ever, the sizes of portions have become huge, even for children. Today, my grandchildren ask for highly advertised, sugar-filled snacks and cereal. Have you looked at food labels lately? Everything has corn syrup . . . pure sugar . . . in it!

Unfortunately, few of us knew any better then, but today—in light of all the information that has become available about food choices and the dangers of obesity, diabetes, early sexual maturation, heart disease, and cancer—many parents are seeking healthier alternatives. A recent study showed that 16 percent of children 6–19 years old are overweight.[1] This is an alarming increase of 45 percent from a similar study conducted in the late '80s to early '90s. Recent research

shows how the development of arteriosclerosis starts with a child's diet. Not only are we beginning to understand that serving our children the foods we grew up on just isn't right any more, we're certainly acknowledging the serious health crisis on our hands. Vegetarian or close-to-vegetarian diets will help children have healthier lives as adults. *Better Than Peanut Butter & Jelly* gives parents, grandparents, and caretakers those healthier choices!

Notes

1. National Health and Nutrition Examination Survey, 1999–2002. http://www.cdc.gov/nchs/products/pubs/pubd/hestats/overwght99.htm (accessed 2005).

# Why Vegetarianism?

There is no greater gift we can give our children than a lifetime of good health. To us, that means establishing good eating habits very early in life. You no doubt have read that there appears to be a link between adult diseases like cancer, heart disease, and stroke, and what we eat as children. The respected child-rearing expert Dr. Benjamin Spock, in the foreword of *Dr. Attwood's Low-Fat Prescription for Kids*, states:

"The process of gradual blocking of the coronary arteries begins not in adulthood but in childhood, even as young as the preschool years . . . The main cause of this arteriosclerosis is the steadily increasing amount of fat in the American diet, particularly 'saturated' animal fats such as those found in meat, chicken, milk and cheeses."[1]

And Dr. Spock even recommends in his 1998 seventh edition of *Dr. Spock's Baby and Child Care* that children be put on a vegan diet. Needless to say, this comment sparked a real debate about the efficacy of vegetarian and vegan diets for children, but a lot of research supports his recommendation. In a position paper on vegetarian diets, the American Dietetic Association concluded, "Appropriately planned vegan and lacto-ovo-vegetarian diets satisfy nutrient needs of infants, children, and adolescents and promote normal growth."[2]

Today, children in the United States get an average of 38 percent of their calories from fat. The American Heart Association, along with the Committee on Nutrition of the American Academy of Pediatrics, recommends that children more than two years old have a total fat intake of no more than 30 percent of the total day's calories, with 10 percent or less from saturated fat. These percentages are easy to achieve by following a vegetarian diet, which is naturally low in saturated fat. We do offer caution regarding the percentage of fat in a child's diet. It is important not to reduce fat below recommended levels for children. A recent study conducted by Judy Driskell, a nutrition scientist at the University of Nebraska, found that preschoolers in her study had low levels of vitamin C, considered linked to low-fat diets. Driskell attributed this to parents sharing their low-fat eating habits with their children.[3]

Another strong reason for becoming partially or fully vegetarian is concern for the environment. We have learned that the relative protein production efficiency for soy is much higher than it is for beef or milk or even wheat. From our literature search:

"One acre of land will support seven people if it is used to grow grains and beans for human consumption; it will support less than one person if that same acre is given over to producing milk and meat."[4]

"It takes just twenty-four gallons of water to produce a pound of potatoes; it takes more than two thousand gallons to produce a pound of beef when you calculate what is needed to grow feed for the steer."[5]

Notes

1. Charles R. Attwood, *Dr. Attwood's Low-Fat Prescription for Kids* (New York: Viking, 1995).

2. V. K. Messina, K. I. Burke, "Position of the American Dietetic Association: Vegetarian Diets," *Journal of the American Dietetic Association* 97 (1997): 1317–1321.

3. "Low Fat Diets May Lack Nutrients for Children," *Washington Post*, April 12, 2005.

4. G. Blix, "Vegetarianism: An Ecological Perspective," *Nutrition 2000 Proceedings* (Loma Linda, CA: Andrews University, 1994).

5. David Pimentel et al., "Water Resources in Food Energy Production," *Bioscience* 32 (1982): 861–867.

# Vegetarianism & Health

There are many positions on diet and perhaps even more diversity in the way people think about vegetarianism today. What was once considered radical in dietary habits is becoming more common in practice, as we better understand human dietary needs. Aiding this understanding is the considerable research on vegetarianism that has been conducted. This research has brought a wealth of new information that helps us better evaluate the vegetarian lifestyle. For instance:

Data show that vegetarians tend to have lower risk throughout their lives for obesity, lung cancer, hypertension, coronary heart disease, and type II diabetes.

Data also suggest that a vegetarian diet may provide lower risk for breast cancer, colonic cancer, osteoporosis, dental erosion, and dental caries.[1]

Vegetarian diets tend to be higher in fiber, the dietary bulk that cannot be broken down by enzymes in the small intestine of the digestive system. Almost all natural fiber comes from plants. Although fiber has little nutritional value, it offers other health benefits. Studies have shown that people with a high-fiber diet experience lower rates of cancer because food passes through the body more rapidly. Because a vegetarian may feel fuller sooner because of the high fiber content of the diet, care must be taken to consume the proper amount of daily calories.[2]

Vegetarians are able to consume enough protein on a daily basis. "It's correct to say that particular combinations of plant foods—e.g., grains + legumes—boost the availability of protein from these foods. But combining foods is no longer something vegetarians need to do to guarantee adequate protein uptake. As long as the vegetarians eat these foods during the course of the day, their protein intake is fine. The secret to getting adequate protein is to eat a variety of foods throughout the day."[3] This means that, rather than worrying about combining certain foods, we will have adequate protein if we ensure that we eat a variety of grains and legumes throughout the day.

Notes

1. "More People Trying Vegetarian Diets," *FDA Consumer* 29 (1995): 10–13.

2. "ADA Position Paper on Vegetarianism," *Journal of the American Dietetic Association* 93 (November 1993): 1317-1319. http://www.vrg.org/nutrition/ada1993.htm (accessed 2005).

3. Vegetarian diet information website, http://www.vegetarian-diet.info/vegetarian-diet-myths.htm (accessed 2005).

# the
# **Nutritional**
# **needs**
# of children

Whatever form of vegetarianism you or your children choose, you need to be aware that the nutritional needs of children are somewhat different from those of adults. To find out just what kids need, we interviewed Randi Cardonick, a registered dietitian with the Hospital of the University of Pennsylvania. A vegetarian and mother herself, Randi told us about the following key vitamins and minerals that should be given special consideration in a child's diet.

**Calcium:** Adequate calcium is needed for strong bones, nerve and muscle function, and blood clotting. Children of different ages need different levels of this nutrient. The latest published requirements at www.keepkidshealthy.com are as follows:

- Toddlers (age 1–3 years): about 500 mg of calcium each day (about 2 glasses of cow's milk).
- Preschool and younger school-age children (age 4–8 years): about 800 mg of calcium each day (about 3 glasses of cow's milk).
- Older school-age children and teens (age 9–18 years): about 1300 mg of calcium each day. This higher level of calcium is especially important once they begin puberty (about 4 glasses of cow's milk).

Calcium-rich foods include calcium-fortified orange juice, fortified soy and rice milk, tofu, oranges, raw broccoli, tahini, figs, raisins, sweet potatoes, black beans, vegetarian baked beans, sesame seeds, almonds, and molasses.

**Iron:** Contrary to popular belief, vegetarian diets are typically high in iron. Iron is found in soy milk, lentils, kidney beans, lima beans, cracked wheat, nuts, bulgur, blackstrap molasses, and spinach. To enhance iron absorption, make sure your kids get plenty of vitamin C. Good sources of vitamin C include broccoli, potatoes, cantaloupe, oranges, cranberry juice, mangoes, strawberries, tangerines, and watermelon. An additional reassurance: "Children who are not meat-eaters get their iron from beans, potatoes, dried fruit, and iron-fortified cereals, and their bodies probably become very efficient at absorbing all the iron they do ingest."[1] Recent studies have found "a vegan child is no more likely to have anemia than an omnivorous child."[2]

**Protein:** Adequate protein intake is important (it helps in the growth and repair of body tissue), and vegetarian diets can provide enough. When children consume enough calories, eat frequently throughout the day, and eat a variety of foods, there's little chance of protein deficiency. The US Recommended Daily Allowance calls for 0.8 gram of protein for each kilogram of ideal body weight. A quick way to calculate this is to divide your child's weight in pounds by 2.75 to obtain his or her RDA in grams. Protein-rich foods include cheese, eggs, beans, peanut butter, tofu, chickpeas, and yogurt, plus grains like quinoa, oats, and wheat.

**Riboflavin:** Riboflavin is important for overall growth and helps produce energy. Cow's milk is high in riboflavin, as are enriched and whole-grains, almonds, almond butter, and avocados.

**Vitamin B12:** Children need 0.7–1.4 micrograms (adults need 2.0) of B12. This vitamin helps the body use protein to build new tissue and to form new red blood cells. Because B12 is mostly found in animal food products, many pediatricians recommend giving supplements to vegan kids. Most brands of fortified soy milk contain B12, but you must check the labels. You can also find breakfast cereals, breads, and crackers that are B12-fortified. A note on vegan diets for children: "With a bit of care a child's protein needs can easily be met on a meatless diet, but it should be noted that a strictly vegetarian diet excluding all meat, eggs, and dairy products is deficient in vitamin B12, making it important for vegan children to be supplemented with this vitamin."[3]

**Vitamin D:** Vitamin D is important for bone formation in children. Most kids get plenty of vitamin D from sun exposure. Other sources include cow's milk, fortified soy or rice milk, and fortified cereals.

**Zinc:** A lack of this mineral can affect growth and sexual maturation in children. Zinc can be found in dairy products, tofu, whole-grains, wheat germ, fortified cereals (bran cereals and oatmeal), nuts, seeds, dried fruit, peas, and legumes.

Notes:

1. Eileen Behan, *Meals That Heal for Babies, Toddlers, and Children* (New York: Pocket Books, 1996), 28.

2. "Iron Status of Vegetarians," *American Journal of Clinical Nutrition,* 1994. *Quoted in The Vegan Child* on website http://www. dieteticintern.com/TheVeganChild.htm (accessed 2005).

3. Barbara Kahan, *Healthier Children: Professional Guidance for Parents in the Area of Nutrition, Environment and Behavior* (Keats Publishing, Inc., 1990), 160. New Canaan, CT.

## Childhood Food Allergies

According to www.keepkidshealthy.com childhood food allergies are less common than thought. About five to eight percent of younger children develop food allergies, but most of them outgrow them by the time they're three years of age. Sometimes intolerance to foods is confused with allergies. Reactions such as diarrhea, vomiting, and rashes could be intolerances and are often linked to a deficiency of the enzyme that breaks down lactose, found in cow's milk.

**Common foods that cause allergies:**

Cow's milk
Eggs
Soybeans
Wheat
Peanuts
Tree nuts (walnuts, pecans, cashews, almonds, and hazelnuts)
Corn
Food dyes and preservatives

If you suspect your child may have a food allergy, check with your doctor.

## Serving Sizes

Adult serving sizes, as suggested by the American Dietetic Association, follow. These portions are appropriate for children older than six who have hearty appetites. For two to five year olds, half of an adult serving is recommended.

**Grains:** 1 slice bread; 1/2 bun, bagel, or English muffin; 1/2 cup cooked cereal, rice, or pasta; 1 ounce dry cereal.

**Vegetables:** 1/2 cup cooked or 1 cup raw.

**Legumes and Meat Substitutes:** 1/2 cup cooked beans; 4 ounces tofu or tempeh; 8 ounces soy milk; 2 tablespoons nuts or seeds.

**Fruits:** 1 piece fresh fruit; 3/4 cup fruit juice; 1/2 cup canned or cooked fruit.

**Dairy Products:** 1 cup low-fat or skim milk; 1 cup low-fat or nonfat yogurt; 1 1/2 ounces low-fat cheese.

**Eggs:** 1 egg or 2 egg whites.

**Fats and Sweets:** to be eaten sparingly.

# The Vegetarian Food Pyramid

The Vegetarian Food Pyramid was developed by the Health Connection, a Maryland-based nutrition education group. It is similar to and may be substituted for the food pyramid offered by the US Department of Agriculture. Fats, sugars, and salt are at the top of the pyramid, meaning they are to be eaten sparingly; grains and cereals are at the broad base of the pyramid to show that they form the basis of a healthy vegetarian diet.

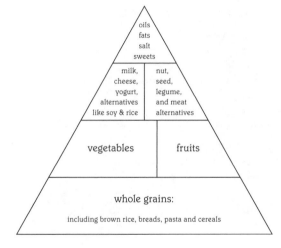

oils
fats
salt
sweets

| milk, cheese, yogurt, alternatives like soy & rice | nut, seed, legume, and meat alternatives |

| vegetables | fruits |

whole grains:
including brown rice, breads, pasta and cereals

**Eat Sparingly:** Vegetable fats and oils, sweets, and salt

**Eat Moderately or 2–3 servings per day:** Legumes, nuts, seeds, and meat alternatives; low-fat or nonfat dairy products and fortified alternatives

**Eat Generously or 5–9 servings per day:** Fruits, vegetables

**Eat Liberally or 6–11 servings per day:** Whole-grain bread, cereal, pasta, and rice

# getting Kids
## to eat well

Start your children young—right when they begin to eat table food—and introduce them to a variety of foods.

Provide a variety of healthy nutrient-rich foods for your child to choose from.

Invite your kids to help with meal preparation. Get them involved with safe cooking methods and safety in the kitchen.

Respect your child's likes as well as dislikes.

Encourage mealtime to be a fun time.

As a parent, set good examples, and be a positive role model. Kids learn food habits from parents.

Never force your children to clean their plates.

Avoid using food as a reward. Food then becomes a comfort and children may then look to food for emotional satisfaction.

If your child doesn't eat much at certain times, don't worry. Her caloric intake will be balanced over a week's time. She may eat "like a bird" one day and "like a horse" on another!

Try to determine what causes your child to refuse certain foods. Are they too hard, soft, cold, hot, or spicy?

Avoid labeling foods as "bad" or "good." It is not a particular food, but a diet over time that influences your child's health.

Kids need to eat often. Be sure snacks are as nutritious as the food you'd serve in a meal.

Let your child fill his own plate from the choices that are available.

Don't forbid certain foods, such as candy or other sweets. It only creates a battleground and makes sweets more appealing than ever!

When you introduce new foods, remember that your children have five senses. Let them feel the food, smell it, fully explore and experience it.

If your child doesn't like what you've prepared for dinner, don't fix him something else. The less attention paid to a missed meal the better off you are. Save the portion for later, when your child announces he is hungry.

Your child probably has some favorite fruits and vegetables. When introducing new food items, serve them with favorites for the pleasant association.

Concentrate on the nutrition your child is getting, not how much food she is eating.

Make whole-grain breads the standard bread in your diet. The extra nutrients will pay off over time.

Limit fruit juice to three or four ounces a day. Don't offer juice before meals, as it may curb appetites.

Talk to your kids about healthy eating. Get them involved in discussions about it. Involve them in making food choices at the grocery store. When you get your children involved with planning and preparation, this helps them to understand the role nutrition plays in their lives.

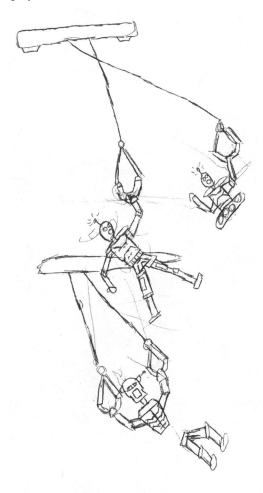

**A *great website*** for current nutritional guidelines is **www.keepkidshealthy.com/ nutrition/vegetarian_diets.html**. Here, you will find good information regarding the amount of calories, fat, iron, and other nutrients that is considered necessary for children's health.

# stocking your
# **Pantry**

It's easy to create a wholesome meal when you have a variety of ingredients available. These are some of the items we recommend always having on hand.

Apple juice

Applesauce, unsweetened

Baking powder

Baking soda

Bananas

Beans, canned: black, fava, kidney, white kidney (also known as cannellini), navy, vegetarian baked, and vegetarian refried

Bulgur wheat (known as kasha or buckwheat groats; great for adding to dishes for extra nutrients)

Canola oil (lowest in saturated fat of all oils)

Carob (a chocolate substitute; virtually fat free, no cholesterol, and low in sodium)

Catsup (sugar free)

Chickpeas (also known as garbanzo beans; a good source of calcium)

Corn, canned

Cornmeal

Cornstarch

Couscous (mixes come in many flavors; use in place of rice or pasta)

Dates (low in fat, high in fiber, and rich in iron and potassium)

Egg Replacer (for those who want to avoid real eggs)

Flour, all-purpose and whole-wheat (combine to get that extra fiber)

Granola

Herbs and seasonings (dried herbs for the pantry; fresh for the refrigerator)

Honey (no fat or cholesterol; wildflower has a wonderful taste)

Jams and jellies, naturally sweetened

Kamut pasta (high-protein pasta; great taste)

Lemon juice

Lentils

Maple syrup

Marinara sauce

Mayonnaise: soy-based

Molasses: blackstrap and regular (blackstrap has a heartier flavor; one tablespoon provides 19 mg calcium and 0.5 mg iron)

Nuts: almonds, peanuts, pecans, walnuts

Okra, canned (high in carbohydrates and fiber; provides some calcium and vitamins A and C)

Olive oil (substantially less saturated fat [14%] than butter [66%]; extra virgin tastes better)

Pancake mix, whole-grain

Pasta, whole-wheat (has five times the fiber of regular white pasta)

Peaches, canned, in unsweetened juice

Peanut butter (no sugar or salt; fresh ground is best)

Picante sauce

Pineapple, canned, in unsweetened juice

Popcorn

Potatoes (store in a cool, dry place)

Pumpkin, canned

Quinoa pasta (ancient Incan high-protein grain; nutty taste; use in place of rice or pasta)

Raisins

Rice, brown

Rice cakes

Rolled oats (high in iron and calcium; don't use instant)

Salsa

Sesame oil

Sesame seeds

Soy sauce, reduced-sodium

Split green peas

Sunflower seeds

Sweet potatoes (store in a cool, dry place)

Taco shells

Tahini (sesame seed butter; for making hummus)

Tamari sauce (a naturally brewed soy sauce with no sugar; interchangeable with regular soy sauce)

Tomato sauce and tomato paste

Tomatoes, canned, crushed, and whole

Tortilla chips, baked

Vegetable broth, canned or bouillon cubes

Vegetable cooking spray, such as Pam

Vinegar: balsamic, rice, and apple cider

Wheat germ (a good source of protein, potassium, vitamin E, iron, folic acid, zinc, and magnesium; sprinkle on casseroles, cereal, veggies)

Wild rice

# stocking your
# Refrigerator

Having a well-stocked refrigerator is a bit more difficult than keeping the pantry shelves full, but most of the following items keep well and are essential to nutritious vegetarian meals.

Apples

Berries, fresh or frozen

Bread, whole-grain

Broccoli (full of anti-oxidants like beta-carotene; high in calcium, vitamin C, and phosphorus.)

Cabbage

Carrots (a rich source of beta-carotene, which our bodies convert to vitamin A, considered to be an anti-cancer agent)

Celery

Cheeses, low-fat: cheddar; Monterey Jack; mozzarella; goat- and sheep-milk cheese, such as feta

Cream cheese, low-fat (also known as Neufchâtel)

Cucumbers (kids may prefer the slightly bitter skin peeled off)

Eggplant

Eggs

Fruit, fresh or frozen

Green beans

Greens: collards, kale, turnip

Herbs: parsley, bay leaves, thyme, rosemary, sage, cilantro, basil

Kefir (a cultured drink made from cow, goat, or soy milk; highly nutritious)

Juice, frozen concentrate

Lemons

Lettuce (the darker green the leaf, the more nutrients; discard outermost leaves of conventionally grown varieties to avoid pesticides)

Limes

Meat substitutes: Yves has numerous meatless products, including hot dogs, burgers, bologna, turkey, salami, casseroles, and so on. Lightlife Foods also has a nice selection of hot dogs, burgers, low-fat "beef" and "chicken" strips. You can buy meatless bratwurst, meatballs, portabella burgers, barbequed ribs, and many other meatless products that taste very good and are either vegetable or soy protein. Many of these products are low-fat and some are vegan.

Mixed vegetables, frozen

Mushrooms: try different kinds, particularly portabellas

Onions

Oranges

Parmesan cheese

Peas: snow, sweet, and snap

Peppers: green and red

Plantains (high in potassium and a good source of vitamin A)

Rice milk

Ricotta cheese, low-fat

Salad dressing, low-fat

Soy milk

Sour cream, low-fat

Spinach, fresh or frozen

Sprouts: try different kinds

Squash: butternut, acorn, and spaghetti

Tofu, water-packed; fresh or boxed; regular or lite. (Tofu is made from soybeans and is easy to digest. It is cholesterol free, low in saturated fat, and a good source of calcium, iron, B vitamins and vitamin E. Soybeans contain 35% usable protein—more than any other unprocessed plant or animal food. Tofu comes in soft, medium, and firm consistencies.)

Tomatoes

Tortillas, whole-wheat

Yogurt

Zucchini squash

# tips for
# Becoming a
# vegan

It is easier than you might think to convert most vegetarian recipes to vegan ones. Generally, you may substitute maple syrup for honey. You may also cut cheese made from cow's, sheep's, or goat's milk from vegetarian recipes and substitute soy cheese. However, the consistency and taste will be affected. You might want to test this first!

**Where eggs are listed as an ingredient, replace with Ener-G Egg Replacer or one of the following ingredients, which are equivalent to 1 egg:**

1 banana (for cake recipes)

2 tablespoons mashed silken tofu

1/4 cup applesauce

**When you wish to replace the dairy in a recipe, substitute:**

Soy milk, rice milk, potato milk, or nut milk (and sometimes water)

Soy cheese

Soy margarine

Soy mayonnaise

Crumbled tofu in place of cottage cheese or ricotta cheese, even in cheesecakes!

Nondairy cream

**When you wish to make a vegan burger:**

Harvest Burger has a vegan version called Grillers Vegan; Boca Burgers also has a vegan version. Check the labels.

**When you wish to use a chicken substitute:**

There are many chicken substitutes on the market these days. Some of them are vegan.

Lightlife Chicken Strips and White Wave Chicken-Style Seitan are both vegan, as are many of the Health Is Wealth varieties. Double check the labels.

**When you wish to use a pre-made pancake, waffle, or baking mix:**

Mixes such as pancake and waffle that do not contain dairy or eggs are usually vegan. Learn to read the labels, however, as some products have animal products when you might assume they do not. On the Internet www.Veg.org is a great resource for additional information.

# Some Vegan Protein Sources:

Adzuki beans

Baked beans

Bean sprouts

Black beans

Black bean sauce

Chana dal

Chickpeas

Kidney beans

Lentils

Mung beans

Nuts: peanuts, cashews, hazelnuts, almonds, walnuts

Oat milk

Peas

Rice milk

Seeds: sesame, sunflower, pumpkin, flax-seed, hemp seed

Seitan

Soy cheese

Soy flour

Soy milk

Soy sauce and miso

Soy yogurt

Soybeans

Tempeh

Tofu

TVP (textured vegetable protein)

Various other milks made from nuts

Whole-grains

Today it is considerably easier to eat vegan because of a much larger choice of foods, both prepared and fresh.

We've labeled each recipe in this book as either vegan or vegetarian:

# Vegan

Recipes contain no animal products.

# Vegetarian

Recipes contain animal products, including dairy products, eggs, or honey.

# quick
# Substitutions

A first step to learning to cook more low-fat, healthful, vegetarian and vegan meals is to start using ingredients that don't contain meat, eggs, dairy products, or refined sugar—or use very little sugar that is raw, called turbinado sugar. Here are some suggestions for substitutions that will work well in most recipes.

| Ingredient | Replace with |
| --- | --- |
| Baked beans, canned (contains pork) | Vegetarian baked beans, canned |
| Beef or chicken broth | Vegetable broth; canned or bouillon cube |
| Butter | Olive oil, sesame oil, Sunsweet, or Lighter Bake |
| Cheeses | Soy- or nut-based cheeses |
| Chocolate | Carob |
| Cold cuts | Tofu "cold cuts" |
| Cottage cheese/ricotta cheese | Crumbled tofu |
| Eggs | Crumbled tofu, soy flour, or Egg Replacer |
| Hamburgers | Veggie burgers |
| Hot dogs | Tofu "hot dogs" |
| Mayonnaise (egg-based) | Soy mayonnaise |
| Milk, cow's | Soy milk, rice milk |
| Oil for baked goods | Applesauce (unsweetened), puréed bananas |
| Oil for sautéing | Vegetable cooking spray, apple juice, vegetable stock |
| Sour cream | Low-fat yogurt, soy yogurt |
| Sugar | Honey, molasses, maple syrup, brown rice syrup, frozen apple juice concentrate |
| Cream | Silken tofu |

# healthy
# Breakfasts

Almost every family has a hard time getting started in the morning. Most of us stay in bed until the last possible minute, then rush through the morning rituals of dressing, packing lunches, finding school books and homework assignments. A morning meal for the kids often means a quick bowl of sugary cereal, a doughnut or toaster pastry on the run, or sometimes nothing at all. Even though we know how important it is for kids to start the day with a nutritious breakfast, many of us wonder how we can possibly find the time to prepare a breakfast, let alone eat one!

But it doesn't have to take a lot of time or effort to get your children off to a healthy start each day. The recipes on the following pages are easy to fix and, for the most part, take no longer than 10 minutes from start to finish. The few recipes that do take longer, such as Banana Bread or Apple-Carrot Muffins, can be made on weekends, or when you have more time, and then frozen for weekday use.

Speaking of time, if you want your children to sit down and eat in the morning, you have to plan for it. Try getting everyone up 15 or 20 minutes earlier each day. This will give you the time you need to fix a good breakfast and allow your children enough time to enjoy it. You could even sit down and have breakfast with them. Chances are everyone will benefit from this healthy start to a busy day.

## Super-Quick Breakfasts

Toast half a whole-wheat English muffin and top with a thin slice of firm tofu, sliced bananas, and strawberries. Sprinkle with granola.

Mix leftover whole-wheat couscous with unsweetened applesauce. Warm briefly in the microwave or in a saucepan. Top with fresh fruit slices, such as orange or banana.

Mash a ripe banana and add a teaspoon of wheat germ. Serve in a cereal bowl with a splash of soy or rice milk. Top with raisins.

Mash leftover cooked butternut squash and mix it with diced apple and a dash of cinnamon. Warm in the microwave or in a saucepan.

Toast half a whole-grain bagel. Top with low-fat cream cheese and sliced banana. Sprinkle with granola.

Take a piece of bread and cut a hole in the middle with a cookie cutter. Fry bread in a pan coated with vegetable cooking spray, then crack an egg and drop into the hole in the bread. Cook until done.

## Fruity Juice

Start any breakfast meal with this refreshing drink.

2 cups orange juice

1 cup pineapple juice

1 orange, peeled, seeded, and sliced

1/2 cup pineapple chunks

In a pitcher, combine juices and stir. Add orange slices and pineapple chunks.

**Vegan. Serves 6.**

# Rice Surprise

Brown rice is just as delicious and nutritious for breakfast as it is for lunch or dinner, and its nutty flavor blends well with the natural sweetness of fruit. It's also a good source of B vitamins, complex carbohydrates, fiber, and protein. We recommend cooking up a big batch of brown rice on the weekend for use during the week. Covered and refrigerated, it will keep 4 to 5 days.

1 cup cooked brown rice

1/2 cup applesauce, unsweetened

1 banana, sliced

In a medium bowl, combine brown rice and applesauce. Cover with wax paper or a paper towel. Heat in microwave for 2 minutes on medium to low setting, stirring once halfway through (or, in a medium saucepan, heat over low heat for 5 minutes). Top with banana.

**Vegan. Serves 2.**

# Tofu Scramble

Turmeric, a yellow-colored spice often used in Indian cooking, helps make this dish look like scrambled eggs. Younger children (or those who don't like "things" in their food) may prefer the recipe without the onion and green pepper. Either way, you'll be surprised this is made from tofu instead of eggs.

1/2 cup onion, chopped

1/2 cup green pepper, chopped

1 clove garlic, minced

1/2 tablespoon olive oil

1/2 pound tofu, firm, crumbled

2 tablespoons nutritional yeast (optional)

1 tablespoon reduced-sodium soy sauce

1/4 teaspoon turmeric

In a medium saucepan, sauté onion, pepper, and garlic in oil until soft. Thoroughly cooked garlic has a mild flavor less likely to be objectionable to kids. Add remaining ingredients. Simmer 2–3 minutes.

**Serving suggestion:** Wrap a generous portion of Tofu Scramble inside warm whole-wheat tortillas and top with picante sauce.

**Vegan. Serves 2–3.**

## Cinnamon-Apple Oatmeal

This is a wonderful alternative to sugar-laden, artificially flavored instant oatmeals. The recipe calls for good old-fashioned rolled oats, not the quick-cooking kind. They taste better, are more nutritious, and they take only a few minutes longer to fix.

1 cup apple juice

1 cup water

1 medium apple, cored and chopped

1 cup uncooked old-fashioned rolled oats

1/4 cup raisins

1/8 teaspoon cinnamon

1/8 teaspoon salt

Slivered almonds

In a medium saucepan, bring apple juice, water, and chopped apple to a boil over medium to high heat. Stir in oats, raisins, cinnamon, and salt until well blended. Cook, uncovered, over medium heat for 5–6 minutes or until thick, stirring occasionally. Spoon into bowls and top with slivered almonds.

**Vegan. Makes 2 generous servings.**

## French Toast

A great starter for kids waking up in the morning after a slumber party!

2 eggs

1 1/2 tablespoons soy or rice milk

2 teaspoons orange juice

1 teaspoon maple syrup

1/8 teaspoon vanilla

1/8 teaspoon ground cinnamon

1 tablespoon margarine

8 slices whole-grain cinnamon-raisin bread

In a medium bowl combine the eggs, soy or rice milk, juice, syrup, vanilla, and cinnamon by beating with a wire whisk. Melt the margarine in a large nonstick skillet over medium heat. Soak bread slices in egg mixture for about 20 seconds on each side and place in skillet. Cook on each side until light brown. Serve with fresh fruit or natural fruit jellies.

**Vegetarian. Serves 8.**

# Berry Breakfast Parfait

Granola has long been considered a "health food," but many of the popular brands contain tropical oils, making them high in saturated fat. You can find low-fat granola on most supermarket shelves these days, but you may have to make a trip to your local whole-foods store to find one that does not contain a lot of refined sugar. For a granola you can trust, try our Make-Your-Own Granola, opposite.

2 cups low-fat vanilla yogurt

1/4 teaspoon cinnamon

1 cup strawberries, sliced

1/2 cup blueberries

1/2 cup raspberries
  (or diced peaches, or blackberries)

1 cup low-fat granola

In a small bowl, combine yogurt and cinnamon. Combine strawberries, blueberries, and raspberries in another bowl. In four serving dishes (clear, tall ones if you have them!) layer 1/4 cup fruit mixture, 2 tablespoons granola, and 1/4 cup yogurt mixture.

**Vegetarian. Serves 4.**

# Make-Your-Own Granola

This simple homemade cereal tastes great alone or with fresh fruit and soy or rice milk. It keeps well in the refrigerator and can be a handy snack food, too, especially with the addition of some raisins or other dried fruit. For a nonfat version, try using a tablespoon of thawed orange or grape juice concentrate in place of the oil.

3 cups uncooked rolled oats
  (not the quick-cooking kind)

1/2 cup sliced almonds

1/4 cup wheat germ

1/4 cup honey or maple syrup

2 tablespoons canola or safflower oil

1/2 teaspoon vanilla

Dash salt

Preheat oven to 300 degrees. In a large bowl, combine all ingredients. Use your hands to mix together. Spread mixture on a cookie sheet that has been lightly coated with vegetable cooking spray and bake 30 minutes, lifting the mixture with a spatula after 15 minutes.

**Vegetarian. Serves 8.**

# Pancakes

We save time by using a complete, whole-grain pancake mix that doesn't require the addition of eggs or milk. You can also use other kinds of mixes or rely on a favorite "from scratch" recipe, then add the fruit and other ingredients listed in each of the recipes below, right before cooking. Whatever your choice, these pancakes-with-extras will give your kids a boost in the morning!

## Banana Pancakes

1 cup multigrain pancake mix

1 cup water

1 teaspoon safflower oil or 1 tablespoon unsweetened applesauce

1 banana, mashed

Cinnamon to taste

1 teaspoon wheat germ (optional)

In a medium bowl, combine the pancake mix, water, and oil. Stir until lumps disappear. Add mashed banana, cinnamon, and wheat germ. Mix until just blended. Spray pancake griddle or frying pan with vegetable cooking spray. Using a high heat setting, cook pancakes on one side until bubbles form on top and edges turn brown. Turn once, and cook a few minutes more. Top with 100 percent fruit syrup, jelly, or fresh berries.

**Vegetarian. Serves 3.**

## Blueberry Granola Pancakes

1 cup multigrain pancake mix

1 cup water

1 teaspoon safflower oil or 1 tablespoon unsweetened applesauce

1 cup blueberries, fresh, or frozen (don't defrost)

1/2 cup low-fat granola

Cinnamon to taste

1 teaspoon wheat germ (optional)

In a medium bowl, combine the pancake mix, water, and oil. Stir until lumps disappear. Add blueberries, granola, cinnamon, and wheat germ. Mix until just blended. Spray pancake griddle or frying pan with vegetable cooking spray. Using a high heat setting, cook pancakes on one side until bubbles form on top and edges turn brown. Turn once. Cook a few minutes more. Top with 100 percent fruit syrup, jelly, or fresh berries.

**Vegetarian. Serves 3.**

**Better than** peanut butter & jelly

# Weekday Waffles

Most busy parents don't have time to make homemade waffles on a weekday morning. But here are two ways to add some variety and extra nutrients to commercially prepared frozen waffles. These recipes are guaranteed to appeal to your kids enough to get them to slow down and eat—even if it's in the car or at the bus stop!

## Peanut Butter & Banana Waffles

4 whole- or multigrain frozen waffles

1/2 cup fresh-ground peanut butter

1 banana, sliced

Toast waffles according to package directions. Spread a layer of peanut butter over each waffle. Top with slices of banana.

**Vegetarian. Serves 2–4.**

## Fruit & Yogurt Waffles

4 whole-grain or multigrain frozen waffles

1/2 cup strawberries, sliced

1/2 cup blueberries

1/2 cup kiwi fruit, sliced

1/2 cup low-fat vanilla yogurt

Toast waffles according to package directions. Top each with even amounts of fruit and a dollop of yogurt.

**Vegetarian. Serves 2–4.**

# Old-Fashioned Sunday Waffles

No child should grow up without knowing what a homemade waffle tastes like or how it feels to anticipate the moment the final product emerges from the waffle iron. Homemade waffles freeze well and can be reheated in the toaster, just like "boughten" ones.

2 cups all-purpose flour, sifted

2 1/2 teaspoons baking powder

3/4 teaspoon salt

2 eggs

1 1/2 cups soy milk

2 tablespoons safflower oil or unsweetened applesauce

Fresh strawberries, washed and sliced

Preheat a waffle iron. Measure 2 cups of sifted flour into a small bowl. Then add the baking powder and salt and sift once more. In a large bowl, beat the eggs with an electric mixer or by hand until they become light yellow. Beat in the milk. Slowly add the dry ingredients and mix until thoroughly blended and smooth. Add the oil or applesauce and blend completely. For each waffle, pour a small amount of batter in the center of the heating plate of the waffle iron. Bake until done. Top with sliced strawberries.

**Vegetarian. Serves 4–6.**

# Breakfast Muffins

There's nothing like the smell of fresh-baked muffins in the morning to perk up a sleepy-headed child.

To save time, dry ingredients can be mixed the night before and then combined with the wet mixture just before baking.

## Banana Muffins

Here's a muffin recipe that doesn't use eggs or milk and yields some of the best muffins we've ever tasted. You'll find them moist, light, sweet, and fluffy.

1/2 cup vegetable oil
3/4 cup maple syrup
3 tablespoons unsweetened applesauce
2 bananas, mashed
1 tablespoon water
2 teaspoons baking powder
1 teaspoon baking soda
2 cups all-purpose flour
Dash cinnamon
1/2 cup chopped walnuts (optional)

Preheat oven to 350 degrees. Spray a 12-cup muffin pan with vegetable cooking spray. Combine all ingredients in a large bowl. Mix until blended. Spoon batter evenly into muffin pan. Bake 20–25 minutes. Remove from pan immediately. Cool on a wire rack.

**Vegan. Makes 12 muffins.**

## Apple-Carrot Muffins

Younger children will enjoy these moist, slightly sweet muffins even more if you bake them in mini-muffin tins. The baking time will be shorter: they're done when a toothpick inserted in the center of a muffin comes out clean. Make extra batches—these muffins freeze well!

3 eggs or equivalent Egg Replacer
1/2 cup honey or maple syrup
1/2 cup unsweetened applesauce
1 cup grated apple
1 cup grated carrot
1 cup whole-wheat flour
1 cup all-purpose flour
2 teaspoons baking powder
1/4 teaspoon salt
1 teaspoon cinnamon

Preheat oven to 375 degrees. Spray a 12-cup muffin tin with vegetable cooking spray. Blend eggs or equivalent, honey, and applesauce until well combined. Stir in apple and carrot. In a separate bowl, sift together flours, baking powder, salt, and cinnamon. Blend dry ingredients with apple mixture until just combined. Spoon into muffin tins and bake 25 minutes.

**Vegetarian. Makes 12 muffins.**

# hearty
# Soups

Soup makes everyone happy. Kids like soup because it's easy for them to eat. Parents like soup because it's easy to serve and a great way to "sneak" vegetables into their children's diet. Take our Creamy Broccoli Soup, for example. Once the broccoli is puréed, we doubt if even the fussiest eater will detect it.

Although we most often serve soup at lunchtime, many of the soups in this chapter are thick and hearty enough to have at dinner as a main course, especially if accompanied with whole-grain bread, a salad, or a side dish. Whenever you make soup, it's a good idea to cook an extra batch to freeze. On busy days when you just don't have the time or energy to cook, you'll be grateful you did.

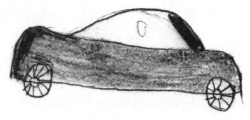

**A note on soup stock:** Traditionally, meat has been used to make stock for soups, but vegetable stock is just as tasty. In addition to being hearty and satisfying, all-vegetable soups often have clear, distinctive flavors that may be masked in soups that depend on chicken or beef broth as a base. Vegetable stock can be made from scratch, but we think many modern parents are just too busy to take this extra step. We use either a canned stock or make ours from vegetable bouillon cubes. Both are available in most grocery stores, shelved with the other soups and broths.

# Creamy Broccoli Soup

This soup gets its creamy texture from puréed vegetables and low-fat soy milk. You may substitute chopped carrots, asparagus, peas, or spinach for the broccoli. Or mix and match!

1/2 onion, chopped

2 cups vegetable broth, canned or from vegetable bouillon cubes

1 cup broccoli, cut into small pieces

1 tablespoon parsley, chopped

1 cup soy milk

Salt and pepper to taste

In a pan sprayed with vegetable cooking spray, sauté onion for 3 minutes or until tender. In a small saucepan, bring vegetable broth to a boil. Reduce heat, add broccoli, and simmer 5 minutes. When the broccoli is tender, place broth and broccoli in food processor with sautéed onions and parsley. Blend until just smooth. Reheat in pan, adding soy milk, salt, and pepper just before serving.

**Vegan. Serves 4.**

# Taco Soup

We took the basic ingredients in a taco, added some extras, and turned it all into soup. Four-and-a-half-year-old Alec told us, "This soup is good!" His mom and dad liked it, too.

1 package (10.5 ounces) tofu, extra-firm, cubed

1 medium onion, chopped

1 medium green pepper, chopped

1 package taco seasoning mix, such as Old El Paso or Taco Bell

1 bottle (1 quart) tomato juice

1 cup salsa

1 cup shredded lettuce

1/2 cup green onion, chopped

1 cup tomato, chopped

1/2 cup low-fat cheddar cheese, grated

Baked tortilla chips

Low-fat sour cream (optional)

Spray a medium saucepan with vegetable cooking spray. Cook tofu, onion, and green pepper over high heat until slightly browned, about 6–10 minutes. Stir in seasoning mix; cook 1 minute. Stir in tomato juice and salsa. Continue cooking, stirring occasionally, until heated through. Ladle soup into bowls; garnish with shredded lettuce, green onion, chopped tomato, cheddar cheese, and tortilla chips. Top with sour cream, if desired.

**Vegetarian. Serves 6.**

**Better than** peanut butter & jelly

## Polka-Dot Pea Soup

Here's a low-fat, milk-free version of creamed pea soup. Serve with a whole-grain bread.

2 cups split green peas, picked over and rinsed

8 cups water

2 carrots, peeled and sliced

1 baking potato, peeled and cubed

Salt and pepper to taste

In a large stockpot, combine all ingredients. Bring to a boil. Reduce heat and simmer for 2 hours. In batches, purée in blender until thick and creamy. Reheat in soup pot. Add salt and pepper to taste.

**Vegan. Serves 8.**

## Black Bean Chili

Serve with Corn Bread from Emily, page 49, and brown rice for a complete meal.

1 medium onion, chopped

2 cloves garlic, minced

1 small zucchini, sliced

1 tablespoon canola oil

1 1/2 teaspoon chili powder, or more to taste

1 teaspoon ground cumin

1 teaspoon dried oregano

1/2 teaspoon paprika

Dash salt

1/4 teaspoon ground red pepper

1 can (15 ounces) black beans, drained and rinsed

4 cups vegetable broth, canned or from bouillon cubes, or water

1 can (14.5 ounces) stewed tomatoes

In a large stockpot, sauté onion, garlic, and zucchini in oil until tender. Stir in chili powder, cumin, oregano, paprika, salt, and red pepper. Cook and stir for 1 minute. Add the beans, broth, and tomatoes. Bring to a boil, reduce heat, cover, and simmer for 1 to 1 1/2 hours.

**Vegan. Serves 8.**

# Potato & Black Bean Soup

This is adapted from a special potato soup Marty's dad used to make.

6 cups vegetable broth, canned or made from bouillon cubes

10–12 medium-sized mushrooms, quartered

1 medium onion, coarsely chopped

1/2 cup carrots, shredded

4 medium potatoes, cut into 1-inch cubes

1 can (15 ounces) black beans, rinsed and drained

1 can (14.5 ounces) whole tomatoes, cut up

1 tablespoon fresh cilantro, chopped

1/2 teaspoon Cajun seasoning

1/2 cup low-fat sour cream or yogurt (optional)

In a large saucepan, combine broth, mushrooms, onion, carrots, and potatoes. Cook over medium-high heat until mixture comes to a boil. Reduce heat to medium, cover, and cook, stirring occasionally until potatoes are just tender; about 10–12 minutes. Stir in beans, tomatoes, cilantro, and seasoning. Cook, stirring occasionally, until heated through. Serve topped with sour cream.

**Vegetarian. Serves 8.**

# Peanutty Soup

We never said we didn't like peanut butter, which in this case adds flavor to this rich and satisfying soup with a West African flair.

1/2 medium onion, chopped

1 garlic clove, crushed

1 tablespoon canola oil

1 can (14.5 ounces) diced tomatoes with juice

1 cup vegetable broth (canned or from bouillon cube)

1 3/4 cups water

1 large sweet potato, peeled and cubed

1/2 cup natural peanut butter

Dash cayenne pepper

Dash salt

1/4 cup cucumber, thinly sliced

1/4 cup peanuts, crushed

1 tablespoon fresh parsley, chopped

In a large soup pot, sauté onion and garlic in oil over medium heat until soft, about 5 minutes. Add tomatoes, broth, water, and sweet potato. Simmer over medium to high heat for 25 minutes. Stir in peanut butter, pepper, and salt. Purée in food processor or blender until smooth and return to pot to warm. Serve sprinkled with thinly sliced cucumbers, crushed peanuts, and fresh parsley.

**Vegan. Serves 6.**

**Better than** peanut butter & jelly

# Fava Bean Soup

This wintertime soup is a great way to introduce children to the rich taste of fava beans, which are fun to eat because they are so big. For a full meal, serve with fresh fruit, warm multigrain bread, and Howlin' Hummus, page 47.

1 can (16 ounces) fava beans, drained and rinsed

4 cups water

1 cube vegetable bouillon
   (or use 1 cup canned vegetable bouillon and reduce water by 1 cup)

1 medium carrot, chopped

1 small onion, chopped

1 clove garlic, minced

1/2 teaspoon dried basil

1 can (14.5 ounces) stewed tomatoes

1 small zucchini, halved lengthwise and sliced

2 ounces whole-wheat spaghetti, broken into small pieces

In a large stockpot, combine drained beans, water, vegetable bouillon cube, carrot, onion, garlic, and basil. Bring to a boil, reduce heat, and simmer for 40 minutes. Add undrained tomatoes, zucchini, and spaghetti. Cook uncovered for 10 minutes or until pasta is done.

**Vegan. Serves 4–6.**

# well-dressed
# Salads

We've come a long way since the days when "salad" referred to iceberg lettuce, a few carrot shreds, and a slice of tomato. Today, we can easily offer our children a wide variety of salad greens and interesting fruits and vegetables to go with them.

We purposely limit the number of vegetables in most of our vegetable salads, since kids are often less receptive to foods that have many things mixed together. For example, we've turned the standard three-bean salad into One-Bean Salad and omitted the onions you would usually find in the standard cucumber salad. But if your kid is a vegetable-lover, go ahead and add some of his or her favorites as you see fit. You'll also find several fruit salads using ingredients from brown rice to tofu and flavorings from honey to curry. Remember, kids love to dip, so you might want to serve salad dressing on the side.

## Super-Quick Salads

Leftover, cooked green beans and sliced mushrooms with oil and vinegar dressing.

Cooked, cold peas with chopped carrots on a bed of lettuce, topped with ranch dressing.

Cold, leftover rice mixed with chopped carrots, tomatoes, green onions, and soy mayonnaise.

Shredded cabbage with chopped green pepper, chopped carrots, and sliced radishes, mixed with ranch dressing.

## Cool Cucumber Salad

Piquant and crisp, this simple salad is good with sliced tomatoes and rye bread.

1 large cucumber, peeled and thinly sliced

4 teaspoons vinegar

1/4 teaspoon salt

Dash pepper

In a medium serving bowl, combine all ingredients. Refrigerate for 1 hour before serving.

**Vegan. Serves 2.**

## Orange & Green Salad

The sesame oil in this salad gives it an interesting flavor. You might not ever think to combine cucumbers, oranges, and peanuts, but we kid-tested it and got favorable reviews.

1 cucumber, peeled and thinly sliced

1 navel orange, peeled and thinly sliced

1 tablespoon peanuts, chopped

1 tablespoon rice vinegar

1 tablespoon sesame oil

Salt and pepper to taste

Combine all ingredients in a serving bowl and chill.

**Vegan. Serves 4.**

## Bulgur Salad

A quick, nutritious salad that you can put together even if the refrigerator's almost empty. Like other grains, bulgur can be stored for up to a year in a closed container kept in a cool, dry place.

1/2 cup bulgur wheat

1 cup water

1 cup romaine lettuce, shredded

1/2 medium tomato, diced

1/3 cup onion, finely chopped

1 tablespoon fresh parsley, chopped

3–4 tablespoons fresh lemon juice

1 tablespoon oil

Dash of salt and pepper

In a small saucepan, bring water to a boil. Add bulgur and let come to a boil again. Turn heat down to the lowest setting and simmer for 15–20 minutes. Remove from heat and let cool. In a medium bowl combine bulgur with lettuce, tomato, onion, parsley, lemon juice, and oil (be sure to add lemon juice before the oil). Mix well. Add salt and pepper to taste.

**Vegan. Serves 4.**

## Eggless Humpty Dumpty Salad

The combination of mashed tofu and turmeric gives this dish the consistency and color of egg salad. In fact, some people won't even notice it has no eggs! Serve by itself, or on toasted whole-grain bread with freshly sliced tomatoes and lettuce for a great-tasting sandwich.

1 package (10.5 ounces) tofu, firm, drained

1 teaspoon apple cider

1 teaspoon vinegar

1 teaspoon honey or other sweetener

1 teaspoon Dijon mustard

1/2 teaspoon turmeric

2 tablespoons celery, diced

1 medium carrot, grated

1 small red pepper, finely minced

1/3 cup sunflower seeds, toasted

1/4 cup soy mayonnaise

Dash pepper and paprika

In a small bowl, mash tofu with a fork. Add remaining ingredients except for mayonnaise and seasonings and mix gently. Add mayonnaise and seasonings, and mix again. Chill.

**Vegetarian. Makes 2 cups.**

# Veggie Salad

This glorious salad is an exception to our limit-the-ingredients advice, but the chickpeas and macaroni give it an everyday look that seems to convince kids it's okay to try. Even if they pick through it and leave little piles of a rejected ingredient or two, consider it a success and next time make it without the "offending" components.

1/2 red pepper, diced

1/2 green pepper, diced

1/2 onion, diced

1 cup broccoli, cut into small florets

2 carrots, diced

1 tomato, diced

1/2 medium zucchini, diced

6 mushrooms, chopped

1/4 cup fresh parsley, chopped

1/8 cup fresh cilantro, chopped

1 can (15 ounces) chickpeas, drained and rinsed

8 ounces elbow macaroni, cooked

3 tablespoons olive oil

1 tablespoon vinegar (flavored, if you prefer)

3 tablespoons low-fat yogurt, plain

Pepper and garlic powder, to taste

In a large bowl, combine all veggies, fresh herbs, chickpeas, and cooked pasta. Drizzle oil and vinegar over mixture and stir well. Add yogurt and stir until mixed. Season with a dash of pepper and garlic powder, if desired. Serve at room temperature or chilled.

**Vegetarian. Serves 6.**

# Mushroom & Bean Salad

This packs well for school lunches. Great with pumpernickel bread!

1 can (15 ounces) navy beans, rinsed and drained

10–12 mushrooms, sliced

1 cup broccoli, cut into small florets

1/4 cup green onions, chopped

1/4 cup fresh basil leaves, chopped

1/3 cup low-fat Italian dressing

Leaf lettuce

In a medium serving bowl, stir together all ingredients except dressing and lettuce. Pour dressing over salad and toss gently. Cover and refrigerate for 30 minutes. Serve over lettuce leaves.

**Vegan. Serves 4.**

## One-Bean Salad

Simple, fast, and very good. Chickpeas (also called garbanzo beans), like most legumes, are a good source of calcium.

2 cans (15 ounces each) chickpeas, drained and rinsed

2 scallions, chopped

1 red onion, diced

1 tomato, chopped

1 garlic clove, crushed

1/4 cup red wine vinegar

2/3 cup olive oil

1/2 cup fresh parsley, chopped

1/4 teaspoon salt

1/8 teaspoon pepper

In a medium bowl, combine all ingredients. Stir, cover, and refrigerate.

**Vegan. Serves 8.**

# Fruit Salads

Kids generally love the flavor and texture of fruit. Here are several fruit recipes to tempt their palates.

To keep cut pieces of apples and bananas from turning brown, quickly toss them with a splash or two of lemon juice.

## Fabulous Fruit Salad

Naturally sweet and delicious, this salad goes with everything.

1/3 cup honey or other sweetener

2/3 cup soy mayonnaise

1/2 cup chopped walnuts

3 medium apples, cored and chopped

2 bananas, peeled and sliced

1 can (10.5 ounces) Mandarin oranges, drained

1 cup seedless grapes, halved

1 tablespoon lemon juice

In a small bowl, blend honey and mayonnaise until smooth. In a separate bowl, combine and toss remaining ingredients. Add honey mixture, stir, and refrigerate until ready to serve.

**Vegetarian. Makes about 7 cups.**

# Brown Rice Fruit Salad

An unusual combination that will surprise your kids with its sweet and refreshing flavors.

## Dressing

1/4 cup low-fat sour cream

1/4 cup low-fat vanilla yogurt

1 tablespoon fresh lime juice

1/2 teaspoon cinnamon

1 teaspoon honey or other sweetener

In a small bowl, stir together all dressing ingredients. Set aside.

## Salad

1 cup brown rice, cooked

1 medium orange, peeled and sectioned

2 medium mangoes, peeled and coarsely chopped

1 medium papaya, peeled, seeded, and coarsely chopped

1 kiwi fruit, peeled and sliced

1 banana, thinly sliced

Halve orange sections, then combine all salad ingredients. Toss with dressing and coat well. Cover and refrigerate at least 2 hours until well chilled.

**Vegetarian. Serves 6.**

# Tofruitti Salad

A great way to introduce curry!

1 package (10.5 ounces) tofu, extra firm, drained

1 cup seedless red or green grapes, cut in halves

1 Red Delicious apple, cored, seeded, and chopped (about 1/2 cup)

1/4 cup celery, chopped

1/4 cup walnuts, chopped

1/4 cup raisins

1/2 cup soy mayonnaise

1/4 teaspoon curry powder

1/4 teaspoon ground ginger

4 lettuce leaves

In a medium bowl, crumble tofu. Add grapes, apples, celery, walnuts, and raisins. In a separate bowl, stir together the mayonnaise, curry powder, and ginger. Add dressing to tofu mixture and stir well. Cover and chill. Spread tofu mixture over lettuce leaves.

**Vegan. Serves 4.**

# Electrifying Fruit Salad

We adapted this ambrosia-like recipe from one that Wendy's Aunt Evelyn serves when her grandchildren, nieces, and nephews come to her house for family get-togethers.

2 Red Delicious apples, peeled and diced

1 can (8 ounces) crushed pineapple with juice

2 bananas, sliced

1 cup seedless red grapes, halved

1 cup seedless green grapes, halved

1 can (6 ounces) orange juice concentrate

1 1/2 orange-juice cans water

In a large bowl, combine all ingredients. Refrigerate.

**Vegan. Serves 6.**

# Side dishes
## for all seasons

Many of the side dishes presented here, such as potato skins, hummus, or Firefighter "French Fries," also make great appetizers or snacks. Others offer new and flavorful ways to prepare cooked vegetables like zucchini and carrots. Kids tend to prefer raw vegetables to cooked, so don't be surprised if you have to coax them to try some of these recipes. Try serving small portions at first, and make sure you've offered other foods. Don't give up if something is shunned the first time around. On another day, your child may be feeling more adventuresome.

Some of the dishes, such as Nutty Beans or Cartwheel Carrots, could be served with brown rice or couscous, whole-grain bread, and a salad to make a full meal.

### Backyard Beans

This dish complements any backyard barbeque.

2 cans (16 ounces each) vegetarian baked beans

1/2 cup catsup

1 tablespoon molasses

1/2 clove garlic, minced

In a medium saucepan, mix all ingredients well. Heat and serve.

**Vegan. Serves 6.**

## Firefighter "French Fries"

Wendy started making these for her vegetarian son when he complained about not being able to eat the food at fast-food hamburger places "like the other kids." Now they are a family favorite, often served alongside meatless burgers for the full "fast food" effect!

Sweet potatoes are one of the stars of the vegetable family. They are packed with vitamins A and C, as well as copper, potassium, and other minerals—and they're a good source of fiber.

2 large sweet potatoes
Vegetable cooking spray

Preheat oven to 375 degrees. Spray a 9 x 12–inch baking sheet with vegetable cooking spray. Peel and slice potatoes into thin horizontal strips to look like French fries. Place potato strips on baking sheet in a single layer. Bake 10 minutes then turn with a spatula. Bake another 10 minutes until crispy and slightly brown.

**Vegan. Serves 2.**

## Sweet Potato Puff

We hope your children like this dish as much as Wendy's son, Sean, did. He once ate half of this casserole by himself—at one sitting! For this recipe, sweet potatoes can be baked in either a conventional or microwave oven.

4 medium yams or sweet potatoes, baked
1 package (10.5 ounces) tofu, soft
1/4 cup honey or other sweetener
2 tablespoons vegetable or canola oil
1/2 teaspoon salt
1 teaspoon cinnamon
1/4 teaspoon nutmeg
1/8 teaspoon ginger

Preheat oven to 350 degrees. Scoop pulp out of baked sweet potatoes and transfer to a blender. Add all other ingredients and blend until smooth. If mixture gets a little too thick, add a few drops of water. Pour in a casserole dish and bake 20 minutes. Serve warm.

**Vegetarian. Serves 6.**

# Howlin' Hummus

Our children howl for more!

1 can (15 ounces) chickpeas, drained with
   liquid reserved

2 tablespoons tahini
   (sesame seed paste)

1 clove of garlic, chopped

Juice of 1 lime

Juice of half a lemon

1/8 teaspoon cayenne pepper

Dash black pepper

In a food processor or blender, combine
chickpeas, tahini, garlic, and lime and
lemon juice. Pulse on and off until chickpeas are coarsely chopped. With processor
running, slowly add enough of the reserved
chickpea liquid to make mixture smooth
and spreadable. Add cayenne and black pepper to taste.

**Vegan. Makes 3 cups.**

**Serving Suggestions:**

Spread 2 tablespoons of Howlin' Hummus
on 2 slices of whole-grain bread. Top with
thinly sliced cucumber and tomato. Cut into
fourths. Or try the ever-popular Lettuce
Wraps, page 62.

Other topping suggestions: bean sprouts,
cheese, thinly sliced leftover veggies, and
thinly sliced or chopped raw carrots. Great
for dipping too!

# Baba Ghanouj

This rivals hummus as a spread, dip, or
snack. The tangy taste of the lemon juice
combined with tahini will make it one of
your child's favorites!

1 medium eggplant

1/2 cup parsley, chopped

1 garlic clove, chopped

1/3 cup tahini

1/3 cup fresh lemon juice

2 tablespoons olive oil

Dash of pepper

Preheat oven to 350 degrees. Place eggplant on a cookie sheet and bake for 1 1/2
hours, or until eggplant begins to collapse.
When cool enough to handle, cut off stem
end and slip off skin. Place eggplant pulp in
a food processor or blender along with the
remaining ingredients, and purée until very
smooth. Serve at room temperature.

**Vegan. Makes about 2 cups.**

# Nutty Beans

This crunchy vegetable dish is as pretty as it is tasty.

1 pound fresh green beans, or 1 package
  frozen (10 ounces)
1/4 cup almonds, slivered
1/4 cup water chestnuts, sliced
Salt and pepper to taste

Cut fresh beans into bite-sized portions. Cook in just enough water to cover until crunchy and just done. Drain, and mix in almonds and water chestnuts. Add salt and pepper to taste.

**Vegan. Serves 6.**

# Stuffed Tomatoes

You can vary this recipe by substituting chopped broccoli or cooked rice for the zucchini.

2 large, ripe tomatoes
1 medium zucchini, chopped
4 ounces low-fat mozzarella cheese, grated
  (optional), plus extra for topping
1/2 cup wheat germ, plus extra for topping
1 tablespoon fresh basil, chopped
Dash salt and pepper
Wheat germ for topping

Preheat oven to 350 degrees. Cut tomatoes in half, crosswise. Scoop out the pulp and juice, leaving an intact shell. Chop tomato pulp and drain. Set aside. Drain tomato shells, cut side down. In a small bowl, mix drained pulp, zucchini, cheese, wheat germ, basil, salt, and pepper. Turn tomato shells over and divide mixture evenly among them. Top with extra grated cheese and sprinkle with wheat germ. Bake for 20 minutes.

**Vegetarian. Serves 4.**

# Corn Bread from Emily

Our friend Emily was asked to give a lesson on Kwanzaa in her son Matthew's first-grade class. She found the original recipe for this corn bread in a book about the African-American holiday and baked it for the class. It was a big hit with the kids! We adapted it for this book, omitting the dairy products and cutting back on the fat. It's perfect with chili or soup.

1 1/2 cups whole-wheat flour

5 teaspoons baking powder

3/4 teaspoon cinnamon

1 cup yellow cornmeal

1/2 cup margarine, softened

1/3 cup honey or maple syrup

3 eggs

3 tablespoons fresh lemon juice

1 cup soy or rice milk

Preheat oven to 350 degrees. Spray two 4 x 8–inch loaf pans with vegetable spray. In a medium bowl, combine flour, baking powder, and cinnamon. Mix well, then add cornmeal and mix again. In a large bowl, beat margarine until smooth. Beat in honey, then add eggs, and lemon juice. Continue beating until mixture is smooth. While beating, add flour mixture and milk, a little at a time. Mix until well blended. Pour into loaf pans and bake for 35–40 minutes. Leave loaves in pans for 5 minutes then remove and transfer to baking racks to cool. This is a very dense bread that will slice better when cool.

**Vegetarian. Makes 2 loaves.**

# Kiddie Kole Slaw

Even if your kids say they "don't like cabbage," they'll love this fresh dish!

1/2 head green cabbage, shredded

1/2 head red cabbage, shredded

2 carrots, peeled and shredded

1/2 green pepper, chopped finely

2 tablespoons parsley, chopped

1/2 cup soy mayonnaise

1 tablespoon vinegar

1 teaspoon honey

Alternate layers of green and red cabbage for a more interesting-looking salad. Use a clear serving bowl and, when layering cabbages, sprinkle carrots, pepper, and parsley into the layers. Mix mayonnaise, vinegar, and honey well, and pour over salad. Serve chilled.

**Vegetarian. Serves 6.**

## Sweet Orange Carrots

Children and adults alike will beg for carrots after they try this.

1 pound fresh carrots, sliced about
 1/4 inch thick, at an angle

1 orange

Salt and pepper to taste

Boil carrots in water until just done but still crunchy; about 10 minutes. Meanwhile, grate rind and squeeze juice from orange, keeping juice and rind separate. Drain carrots and add orange juice. Allow to sit for 5 minutes. Add rind, salt, and pepper.

**Vegan. Serves 6.**

## Zany Zucchini

Add salad and crusty whole-grain bread for a quick lunch.

2 medium-sized zucchini squashes, thinly
 sliced

1/4 cup grated Parmesan cheese

In a medium nonstick saucepan sprayed with vegetable cooking spray, sauté zucchini slices until crisp-tender, about 2 minutes. Coat with Parmesan cheese and serve immediately.

**Vegetarian. Serves 2–3.**

## Cartwheel Carrots

Your kids will "flip" over these slightly sweet veggies. Serve over whole-wheat couscous with a fresh green salad.

2 cups carrots, sliced

3/4 cup apple juice

1 teaspoon grated orange peel

1 teaspoon grated lemon peel

1 tablespoon honey or other sweetener

1/2 teaspoon cornstarch

In a small saucepan over medium heat, combine carrots and apple juice. Cover and simmer 10 minutes, or until carrots are tender. If liquid evaporates, add a small amount of water. Uncover pan and add remaining ingredients. Simmer, uncovered, 3–5 minutes, or until liquid is thick. Serve hot.

**Vegetarian. Serves 3–4.**

# Stir-Fried Green Beans with Peanuts

What a perfect combo—peanut butter and veggies! This will get your kids to finally eat their vegetables.

Green beans should be cooked just till they turn bright green to keep their pleasing crunchiness; if beans turn dull colored, they are overcooked.

1/3 cup water

8 ounces green beans, fresh or frozen

3 tablespoons reduced-sodium soy sauce

1 tablespoon honey or other sweetener

1/8 teaspoon garlic powder

1 tablespoon peanuts, chopped

In a medium frying pan or wok, bring water to a boil. Add green beans and cook until most of the water has evaporated. Add soy sauce, honey, and garlic powder. Stir rapidly over high heat for 1 minute or until green beans are coated. Transfer to a serving platter and top with chopped peanuts.

**Vegetarian. Serves 3–4.**

# Crispy Snow Peas

Kids prowling the kitchen asking when dinner will be ready? Hand them a raw snow pea for a snack and watch them ask for more!

2 teaspoons sesame oil

1 pound snow peas, stems removed

1 can (8 ounces) sliced water chestnuts, drained

1/2 teaspoon fresh ginger, minced

1 tablespoon low-sodium soy sauce

In a large nonstick skillet or wok, heat the sesame oil over high heat until it starts to sizzle. Add snow peas, water chestnuts, ginger, and soy sauce. Stir-fry for 3–5 minutes or until peas are crispy-done.

**Vegan. Serves 4.**

## Fancy Plantains

The plantain is a wonderful fruit often used in Cuban or Caribbean dishes. Plantains look somewhat like bananas but must be cooked before eating. At the store, choose green-skinned ones that have some black dots; they'll be ripe and ready to cook. The slightly sweet flavor of plantains is especially good with rice and black beans.

1 large plantain, peeled and sliced
1 tablespoon honey or other sweetener

Spray a medium nonstick saucepan with vegetable spray, and sauté plantain slices until tender. Coat with honey and serve warm.

**Vegetarian. Serves 2.**

## Broccoli with Sesame Seeds

An easy way to dress up this everyday veggie. Sesame seeds add great taste and are among the lowest in fat of all the nuts and seeds.

2 tablespoons sesame seeds
2 cups broccoli, cut in pieces
1/4 cup water
1 clove garlic, minced

Preheat oven to 350 degrees. On an ungreased cookie sheet, bake sesame seeds until golden brown, about 10 minutes. Place broccoli in a microwave-safe dish, add water, and cover tightly. Microwave on high for 4 minutes. Let stand 2 minutes. (Or steam broccoli in a saucepan until tender.) Drain and toss with baked sesame seeds and minced garlic.

**Vegan. Serves 2–3.**

# Potatoes

Potatoes are nothing short of glorious for the family kitchen. They are inexpensive, nutritious, easy to prepare in endlessly delicious ways, and a perennial favorite with children. Potato skins have a considerable amount of fiber, iron, and potassium. If you eat both the insides and the skin, you'll get almost double your intake of these nutrients, according to the website www.MayoClinic.com. We recommend using organic potatoes since potatoes receive more chemicals than any other crop, according to the US Department of Energy, and their skins are the hardest to clean of any vegetable.

Baked potatoes are a staple in our households: good alone for lunch or as a side dish with dinner. Before baking them, be sure to scrub raw potatoes well with a brush under cold running water. Pat dry and prick each potato several times with a fork. Bake in a microwave or conventional oven.

**Microwave:** Bake on high for 6–7 minutes. Test for doneness. Continue to bake in 1-minute increments until potato is soft when pierced with a fork. For moister potatoes, wrap in aluminum foil for 5 minutes after removing from the microwave.

**Oven:** Bake potato at 350 degrees for about 1 hour. For enhanced flavor, wrap the potato and a small piece of bay leaf in aluminum foil before baking.

# Grandma's Great Potato Salad

Marty's grandmother made the best potato salad: chunky, tasty, and filling. This is an adaptation of that old Missouri farm-style salad.

6 medium potatoes, peeled and cut in cubes

1/2 green pepper, chopped

2 stalks celery, finely diced

1/2 onion, chopped

1/2 cup soy mayonnaise

1/4 cup Dijon mustard

1 tablespoon vinegar

1 garlic clove, minced

Salt and pepper to taste

2 tablespoons sunflower seeds

In a medium saucepan, boil potatoes until tender, about 20 minutes. Drain and mix in a medium bowl with chopped pepper, celery, and onion. In a small bowl, combine mayonnaise, mustard, vinegar, and garlic, and pour over potato mixture. Stir gently until vegetables are well coated. Add salt and pepper. Top with sunflower seeds.

**Vegan. Serves 6.**

## Tofu Spuds

The addition of tofu makes this baked potato doubly nutritious and very filling.

1 baking potato

1/4 cup tofu

1/8 cup cheddar cheese, shredded

1 tablespoon soy or rice milk

1 tablespoon grated Parmesan cheese

Bake potato and slice in half lengthwise. Scoop out most of the inside, preserving the shells, and mash well. Mash tofu and fold into mashed potato. Add cheddar cheese and milk. Whip with an electric mixer until fluffy. If the mixture is too dry, add more milk. Fill potato shell with mixture and place on baking sheet. Top with grated Parmesan cheese. Bake at 350 degrees until browned and crusty, about 10–15 minutes.

**Vegetarian. Serves 2.**

## Baked Potato with Carrots

Use any and all leftover veggies for this one.

1 baking potato

1–2 carrots

1 tablespoon soy or rice milk

1 tablespoon cooked peas or cooked, chopped broccoli

Bake potato and slice in half lengthwise. Scoop out most of the inside, preserving the shells, and mash well. Cut carrots into 1/2-inch slices and boil in water until soft. Mash the carrots well, then combine with mashed potato. Add soy milk and stir until blended. Return mixture to preserved shell and re-heat. Top potato with a spoonful of warm cooked peas or broccoli.

**Vegan. Serves 2.**

**Better than** peanut butter & jelly

# Marvelous Mashed Potatoes

A dairy-free version of mashed potatoes.

3/4 cup soy milk

Pulp from potatoes for Prize-winning Potato Skins, page 56, or 4 potatoes, peeled, cubed, and boiled until well done

1 teaspoon olive oil

1 clove garlic, minced

In a small saucepan, heat soy milk over low heat. With an electric mixer, blend reserved pulp of potatoes or cooked, cubed potatoes. Slowly blend in heated soy milk, olive oil, and garlic. Serve immediately.

**Vegan. Serves 4.**

# Italian-Style Potatoes

Serve with steamed green beans for a complete meal.

2 large baking potatoes

1 tablespoon olive oil

1 clove garlic, chopped

1/2 green pepper, cut into thin strips

1/2 teaspoon salt

1/2 teaspoon oregano

Dash pepper

1 cup canned tomatoes, peeled and diced

2 tablespoons tomato paste

1 cup mozzarella cheese, shredded

Cut unpeeled potatoes into thin slices, barely 1/8 inch thick. Heat oil in a 10-inch skillet, and sauté garlic, pepper, and potatoes over medium heat. Stir occasionally, until potatoes begin to turn transparent, about 5 minutes. Add seasonings, tomatoes, and tomato paste. Cover and simmer over low heat until tender, 30–45 minutes. Stir once or twice during cooking so potatoes are evenly cooked. Remove from heat, top with cheese, cover and let stand for one to two minutes or until cheese melts.

**Vegetarian. Serves 6.**

## Prize-Winning Potato Skins

Organic potatoes only, please! Chemicals used in growing potatoes are most concentrated in the skins.

5 potatoes
1/3 cup low-fat cheddar cheese, shredded
Olive oil

Preheat oven to 400 degrees. Bake potatoes for 1 hour or until soft when pierced by a fork. Cool. Preheat broiler. Split each potato lengthwise into halves. Scoop out pulp with spoon, leaving a 1/4-inch shell (save pulp for Marvelous Mashed Potatoes, page 55). Brush the insides of the potato skins lightly with olive oil and place them, skin-side down, on a baking sheet. Broil about 6 inches from heat for 5 minutes or until lightly browned and crisp. Reset oven to 350 degrees. Sprinkle skins with cheese and bake about 10 minutes or until cheese melts. Serve with salsa on the side.

**Vegetarian. Yields 10.**

## Baked Potato with Cream Cheese & Salsa

Add a Mexican flavor to baked potatoes. This is terrific with a green salad for a healthy, light lunch.

1 baking potato
2 teaspoons low-fat cream cheese (Neufchâtel)
2 teaspoons salsa

Bake potato and slice in half lengthwise. Scoop out most of the inside, preserving the shells. Mash the removed potato with 1 teaspoon salsa. Return mixture to shells and top with the low-fat cream cheese and remaining salsa. Serve immediately.

**Vegetarian. Serves 2.**

# Sandwiches and packables

There's no denying the ease of slapping a few pieces of bologna or turkey between two slices of bread, or mixing tuna and mayonnaise for tuna "salad" sandwiches, and calling it lunch. But for those of you who are concerned about better nutrition, especially if your kids don't eat meat or fish, preparing a sandwich or packable lunch can be more of a challenge.

So what kind of meatless sandwiches can you prepare for your child to eat at home or take to school? Part of the reason we wrote this book was that other cookbooks didn't seem to answer this question. We finally developed the recipes that follow, paying particular attention to making them easy to prepare and pack. Some of the recipes (Lettuce Wraps, for example) are even easy enough for your children to prepare by themselves. You may have noticed—we certainly have—that children who help make their own meals are more likely to eat them.

If you haven't added tortillas and pita breads to your sandwich repertoire, now's the time. Proven kid-pleasers, they come in whole-wheat varieties for more fiber and vitamins.

For hot meals, be sure to check out the soup recipes in the Hearty Soups chapter. Packed in a wide-mouthed thermos, soup makes an excellent lunch-to-go.

## Falafel Sandwich with Lemon-Tahini Dressing

Falafel is a popular Middle Eastern dish made from chickpeas. Traditionally, the chickpea mixture is formed into small balls (like meatballs) that are deep fried. Here, we flatten out the balls to create little patties that can be cooked in just a small amount of oil. The Lemon-Tahini Dressing adds just a little zing.

### Lemon-Tahini Dressing

3/4 cup low-fat yogurt, plain

1/4 cup tahini

Juice from half a lemon

In a small bowl, mix ingredients well. Set aside.

### Falafel Filling

1 cup canned chickpeas, drained and rinsed

1/3 cup water

1/2 cup wheat germ

1 tablespoon tahini

1 tablespoon lemon juice

1 tablespoon tamari

1 teaspoon cumin

1/2 teaspoon chili powder

1/2 teaspoon turmeric

1 tablespoon whole-wheat flour

In a food processor or blender, purée chickpeas and water until smooth or nearly so. Stir in remaining ingredients; mix well (the mixture will be soft). Form the mixture into 1-inch balls. Lightly oil a large skillet. Place the balls in the skillet and flatten into patties with a spatula. Cook over medium heat 8–10 minutes.

To assemble, spread dressing mixture inside one half of a whole-wheat pita pocket, add shredded lettuce, chopped cucumber, carrot shreds, sprouts, and warm falafel.

**Vegetarian. Serves 4.**

## Mexican Pizza Sandwich

This is a good recipe to let little ones make themselves.

1/2 cup shredded cheese of your choice

1 tomato, chopped

1 teaspoon olive oil

1/2 cup salsa

Chopped cilantro for garnish (or 1/2 teaspoon dried)

2 whole-wheat tortillas

Mix cheese, tomato, olive oil, salsa, and cilantro. Spread over tortillas. Broil on low until bubbly and slightly browned. Serve with fresh fruit.

**Vegetarian. Serves 2.**

# Carrot Salad Pita

If you're going to send this sandwich to school with your child, it's a good idea to pack the pita bread separate from the salad. Slice the top off the pita before you pack it so your youngster can stuff the pocket at lunchtime.

1 small can (8 ounces) pineapple chunks packed in juice, drained

2 carrots, grated

1/2 cup raisins

1/2 cup walnuts

1 teaspoon canola oil

Splash of cider vinegar

4 whole-wheat pitas

In a medium bowl, combine pineapple, carrots, raisins, walnuts, oil, and vinegar. Divide evenly and stuff into pitas just before serving.

**Vegan. Serves 4.**

# Tomato-Basil Pita

This is great for a picnic lunch. Pack marinade separately and pour on sandwiches just before eating. Or save some time by marinating the tomatoes and mozzarella a day in advance. For a delicious "salad" pita, omit the cheese.

4 small ripe tomatoes, thinly sliced

4 ounces mozzarella cheese, cut into 8 slices

1/4 cup fresh basil, chopped

1/3 cup red-wine vinegar

1 teaspoon grated lemon rind

1 clove garlic, minced

Salt and pepper to taste

4 whole-wheat pitas

4 lettuce leaves

In a shallow serving dish, arrange tomato and mozzarella slices. In a small bowl, combine basil, vinegar, lemon rind, garlic, and salt and pepper to taste. Drizzle over tomatoes and cheese. Cover and chill for 1 hour. Split open pitas and line each with a lettuce leaf. Fill each with four slices of tomato and two slices of cheese. Sprinkle marinade over tomato and cheese filling.

**Vegetarian. Serves 4.**

# Grilled Cheese
## with Apple Slices

A healthier alternative to the usual high-fat grilled cheese sandwich. The apples add crunch and a natural sweetness.

2 ounces cheddar cheese, grated

Pinch of ground cinnamon

Pinch of ground nutmeg

Enough canola or safflower oil to brush outsides of bread

4 slices whole-wheat bread

1/2 small Granny Smith apple, peeled and sliced

In a small bowl, combine cheese and spices and mix well. Brush oil on one side of each slice of bread. Place two slices, oil side down, on griddle. Top with cheese mixture and apple slices. Top with remaining slices of bread, oil side up. Turn several times with a spatula until both sides are toasted and cheese is melted.

**Vegetarian. Serves 2.**

# The Vegetarian Club

This takeoff on the traditional club sandwich is perfect for kids.

3 slices whole-grain bread, toasted

1/2 cucumber, peeled and thinly sliced

2 slices low-fat Monterey Jack cheese

1/2 cup alfalfa sprouts

1/2 tomato, thinly sliced

2 lettuce leaves

1 tablespoon soy mayonnaise

Top one toast slice with half of all ingredients. Top with another toast slice, then rest of ingredients. Top with third slice. Cut sandwich diagonally into quarters.

**Vegetarian. Serves 2.**

# Where's-the-Tuna Salad Sandwich

For real ex-tuna lovers, this will taste just enough like the old favorite to be highly satisfying. It's also much lower in fat! The dried, powdered kelp, available in some large grocery stores and health food stores, contains more minerals than any other food. It tastes salty and is often used as a seasoning ingredient or a substitute for salt.

1 can (15 ounces) chickpeas, rinsed and drained

1/4 cup celery, finely chopped

1/4 cup onion, finely chopped

1 tablespoon lemon juice

2 tablespoons soy mayonnaise

1 tablespoon parsley, chopped

1 1/2 teaspoons dried, powdered kelp

Salt and pepper to taste

In a medium bowl, mash the chickpeas with a fork. Add the remaining ingredients and mix well. Serve on whole-wheat toast or fresh rye bread.

**Vegan. Serves 3.**

# Where's-the-Chicken Salad Sandwich

This sandwich is delicious and tastes remarkably like chicken.

1/4 cup fat-free sour cream

1 tablespoon soy mayonnaise

1/4 teaspoon curry powder

2 cups meatless chicken pieces, chopped

1/3 cup celery, chopped

2 tablespoons dry-roasted cashews, chopped

1 tablespoon green onions, finely chopped

2 (2-ounce) whole-wheat hamburger buns

Combine first 3 ingredients in a large bowl, stirring until well blended. Add "chicken," celery, cashews, and green onions; stir well. Serve "chicken" salad on buns.

**Vegetarian. Serves 4.**

# Lettuce Wraps

These inside-out sandwiches make great finger food for kids of all ages. Once you see how popular they are, you'll probably invent your own fillings. Serve with salad dressing for dipping.

1 cup Howlin' Hummus, see page 47

1/4 cup red pepper, chopped

1/4 cup carrots, shredded

1/4 cup cucumber, shredded

4 large lettuce leaves

In a medium bowl, combine hummus with the chopped red pepper. Spread 1/4 on each leaf, and top with carrot and cucumber shreds. Roll leaf up into an egg-roll shape.

**Vegan. Serves 4.**

# Tofu Spread

Our friend Theresa shared the recipe for this delicious spread with us. Use it to top whole-grain breads, bagels, and crackers, or as a dip for fresh vegetables. It will keep in the refrigerator for up to two weeks.

2 cups chunky applesauce, unsweetened

1 package tofu (10.5 ounces), soft, drained

1/2 cup low-fat yogurt; plain, vanilla, or lemon

3 tablespoons honey

3 tablespoons fresh lemon juice

1 teaspoon cinnamon

1 teaspoon nutmeg

2 tablespoons tahini

2 teaspoons vanilla

4 teaspoons whole-wheat pastry flour

1/2 cup raisins

1/2 cup slivered almonds

Preheat oven to 350 degrees. Spray baking dish with vegetable cooking spray. In a food processor or blender, blend all ingredients. Pour into pan and bake for 30–40 minutes or until the top starts to brown. Remove from oven and let cool. Makes great sandwiches, open-faced or closed.

**Vegetarian. Serves 10.**

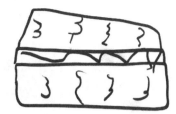

## Veggie Burgers

If your kids crave burgers, try one of the many varieties of frozen veggie burgers that have come on the market over the years. Be sure to read the nutritional information on the boxes, though—some brands are high in fat. We like Boca Burgers No Fat veggie burgers, which taste almost like conventional burgers. Use your imagination here and add whatever strikes your kid's fancy. It's a great way to combine a healthy array of veggies.

2 veggie burgers

2 whole-grain hamburger buns

2 lettuce leaves

2 ripe tomato slices

1 avocado, sliced

2 slices red onion

1/2 cup bean sprouts

Catsup and mustard to taste

Cook veggie burgers according to package directions. Meanwhile, warm buns in oven. Divide other ingredients evenly as burger toppings.

**Vegetarian. Serves 2.**

## Asparagus & Tofu Salad Sandwich

This light vegetable blend is surprisingly appealing.

8 spears fresh asparagus, broken into 1-inch pieces

1 package (10.5 ounces) tofu, firm, crumbled

2 green onions, finely chopped

1/4 cup soy mayonnaise

1 teaspoon fresh dill, finely chopped

1 teaspoon Dijon mustard

1/2 teaspoon lemon juice

Dash pepper

1 cup alfalfa sprouts

4 whole-grain bagels, halved

Sunflower seeds, salt-free (optional)

In a saucepan, cook asparagus in a small amount of water for 2–3 minutes, or until tender. Drain and rinse under cold water to stop cooking process. In a large mixing bowl, combine asparagus, tofu, and green onions. In a separate small bowl combine mayonnaise, dill, mustard, lemon juice, and pepper. Add dressing to asparagus-tofu mixture and mix well. Place alfalfa sprouts on each bagel half. Spoon asparagus mixture over sprouts. Top with sunflower seeds, if desired.

**Vegan. Serves 4.**

# Meatless Sloppy Joes

Another "normal" meal to keep vegetarian kids from feeling different.

1 clove garlic, minced

1/2 onion, chopped

2 cups ground meat substitute, crumbled

3/4 cup tomato sauce

1/4 cup water

1/3 cup barbecue sauce

1 teaspoon chili powder

1/4 teaspoon cumin

4 hamburger buns or hard rolls

Spray a large skillet with vegetable cooking spray. Add garlic and onion. Sauté over medium heat until onions are soft (add a little water to the skillet if onions start to stick). Add meat substitute, tomato sauce, water, barbecue sauce, chili powder, and cumin. Stir to combine. Bring to a boil and then simmer for 5 minutes. Divide mixture evenly onto 4 hamburger buns or hard rolls.

**Vegetarian. Serves 4.**

# Spinach Sandwich

If your child doesn't like the taste of raw spinach, substitute red leaf lettuce.

1/2 cup low-fat cream cheese (Neufchâtel)

1 teaspoon fresh dill

1 carrot, grated

4 slices whole-wheat bread

4 fresh spinach leaves

1 ripe tomato, thinly sliced

Mix cream cheese, dill, and carrot until smooth. Spread over two slices of bread. Cover with two spinach leaves and a few tomato slices and top each with another slice of bread.

**Vegetarian. Serves 2.**

# tempting
# Main dishes

The following recipes will come in handy on those evenings when you're tired, it's late, you're faced with fixing another meal, and your children are clamoring, "Mom! Dad! I'm hungry! When's dinner going to be ready?"

Most of the entrées and one-dish meals in this chapter are quick and easy to prepare. To make them even easier, chop your vegetables in advance and store them in plastic bags in the refrigerator. Or assemble the casseroles a day or two in advance so they're ready to pop in the oven as soon as you get home. While they're cooking, you'll have time to catch up with your family, help with homework, and maybe even relax a bit.

And for those evenings when you're truly pressed, here are some suggestions for super-quick main meals.

## Super-Quick Main Dishes

Mix leftover pasta with frozen or chopped, fresh vegetables and low-fat marinara sauce. Top with wheat germ; heat in the oven or microwave.

Mix cooked whole-wheat couscous with stewed tomatoes, chickpeas, and cooked carrots; heat in the oven or microwave.

Mix leftover brown rice with lima beans and grated cheddar cheese; bake with a bread-crumb topping.

Heat leftover brown rice and serve with canned black beans and Fancy Plantains, page 52. Or for another high-protein rice-and-beans favorite, heat canned kidney beans with a cup of mild salsa in a saucepan and serve over cooked brown rice.

Take a whole-wheat tortilla, and spread with vegetarian refried beans or any other canned beans, chopped tomato, or leftover cooked veggie, and sprinkle with grated cheese. Heat in the oven or microwave until cheese melts. Top with mild salsa.

Steam 3 cups of broccoli florets and serve over polenta made from a mix (we like Fantastic). Drizzle with a small amount of olive oil.

## Southwestern Pasta Casserole

This is a very high-protein, low-fat meal that looks and tastes as good as another kid-favorite, macaroni and cheese. Serve with a whole-grain bread and fresh or frozen peas.

1 package (12 ounces) quinoa pasta (or other high-protein pasta)

1/2 cup soy milk

1 tablespoon cornstarch

10 ounces low-fat cheddar cheese, grated

1/4 cup low-fat sour cream (optional)

4 ounces mild green chilies, chopped

1/2 tomato, finely chopped

4 ounces black olives, chopped (optional)

1/2 cup crushed corn flakes or wheat germ

Preheat oven to 350 degrees. Cook pasta according to package directions. Drain and set aside. Combine soy milk and cornstarch in a small saucepan. Stir over low to medium heat until thickened. Stir in cheese, sour cream, chilies, tomato, and olives. Mix until cheese melts. Add cheese mixture to pasta. Pour into 8-inch square baking pan sprayed with vegetable cooking spray. Sprinkle corn flakes or wheat germ over the top. Bake, uncovered, for 30 minutes until bubbly and browned.

**Vegetarian. Serves 4.**

# Tofu Stir-Fry

Stir-frying is a Chinese style of cooking that allows you to cook a lot of food in very little oil. The trick is to chop ingredients into small pieces and continuously toss and stir them over very high heat. Woks are great for stir-frying. Their rounded sides allow the food to cook evenly. If you don't have a wok, a large skillet or frying pan will work, too.

1/2 cup vegetable broth or water

1/2 cup orange juice

2 tablespoons reduced-sodium soy sauce

4 teaspoons cornstarch

1 tablespoon canola or olive oil

2 teaspoons ginger root, freshly grated

1 clove garlic, minced

2 carrots, peeled and sliced into 1/4-inch pieces

1 small red pepper, sliced

1 small green pepper, sliced

2 green onions, chopped

1/2 cup broccoli florets

1 small, yellow summer squash, sliced into 1/2-inch thick rounds

1 package (10.5 ounces) tofu, extra firm, drained and cut into 1/2-inch cubes

1/2 cup pine nuts

Dash pepper

Dash salt

2 cups cooked brown rice

In a small bowl, combine broth, orange juice, soy sauce, and cornstarch. Stir to dissolve cornstarch. Set aside.

In a large nonstick skillet or wok, heat oil over high heat. Add ginger root and garlic. Stir-fry over high heat 1 minute. Add carrots and stir-fry 3 more minutes. Add peppers, onions, broccoli, and squash. Stir-fry 3 more minutes. Remove vegetables and set aside. Add tofu to pan and gently stir-fry for 2 to 3 minutes until lightly browned. Remove from pan.

Stir the soy sauce mixture and add to pan. Cook, stirring, until sauce is thickened and bubbly. Return vegetables and tofu to pan. Add pine nuts and stir to coat with sauce. Cook, covered, 1 minute or until heated through. Salt and pepper to taste. Serve over rice.

**Vegan. Serves 4.**

## Potato & Leek Casserole

Leeks are among the finest and least-appreciated veggies of all. Your kids will love this dish and their veggie IQ will rise accordingly! If you've never bought or cooked leeks before, here are some tips. They look like giant scallions. You'll want to trim off the green leaves at the top and the white roots at the bottom, just as you do with scallions. Remove the outer membrane, rinse thoroughly because dirt and sand get embedded between layers, then slice.

2 medium leeks, sliced thinly

3 cups mushrooms, sliced

1 cup low-fat mozzarella cheese, grated

3/4 cup low-fat ricotta cheese

1 clove garlic, crushed

Dash pepper

3 cups potatoes, sliced, skin on, and
    partially cooked

1/2 cup wheat germ

1 tablespoon canola oil

1/4 cup low-fat sour cream (optional)

Preheat oven to 425 degrees. In a large non-stick skillet, sauté leeks and mushrooms until crisp-tender. In a small bowl, combine mozzarella, ricotta, garlic, and pepper. Spray a casserole dish with vegetable cooking spray. Arrange 1 cup potatoes over the bottom. Spoon 1/3 of leek-mushroom mixture over potatoes. Cover with 1/3 cup of the mozzarella-ricotta cheese mixture. Repeat layers. Top with wheat germ. Drizzle oil over top. Bake for 1 hour until potatoes are tender and browned. Serve with sour cream, if desired.

**Vegetarian. Serves 4.**

## Couscous with Chickpeas & Carrots

Couscous is a terrific alternative to rice. The combination of nutty-flavored chickpeas with carrots makes a great meal.

4 carrots, peeled and sliced into
    1/4-inch pieces

1 can (15 ounces) chickpeas, drained and
    rinsed

4 cups cooked whole-wheat couscous

Salt and pepper to taste

Spray a large nonstick skillet with vegetable cooking spray. Add carrots and sauté until just tender. In a large serving bowl, combine carrots, chickpeas, couscous, salt, and pepper. Serve warm.

**Vegan. Serves 6.**

# Veggie Burritos

This dish is a healthy way to serve burritos and well worth the time it takes to prepare!

1 can (15.5 ounces) red kidney beans, drained (reserve liquid and rinse beans)

1 1/2 teaspoon chili powder

1/2 teaspoon garlic powder

1/2 cup corn, frozen or canned, drained

6 whole-wheat tortillas

1/4 cup onion, thinly sliced

1 small green pepper, thinly sliced

1 small red pepper, thinly sliced

1 1/2 tablespoons lemon juice

1/4 cup salsa

1 cup fresh tomatoes, diced

1/2 cup low-fat cheddar, Monterey Jack, or soy cheese, grated

Low-fat sour cream (optional)

Preheat oven to 350 degrees. In a food processor or blender, combine beans, reserved bean liquid, chili powder, and garlic powder. Process until smooth. Place bean mixture in a bowl; add corn and stir. Set aside.

Stack tortillas on a microwave-safe plate; wrap in damp paper towels and microwave on high for 20 seconds. Spread 1/4 cup of bean mixture down center of each tortilla. Fold in opposite sides, then top and bottom of tortilla. Place, seam side down, in a square baking pan sprayed with vegetable cooking spray. Cover and bake 15–20 minutes or until heated through.

Meanwhile, spray a large skillet with vegetable cooking spray. Sauté the onion, green and red pepper, and lemon juice over medium heat for about 5 minutes or until vegetables are crisp-tender. Reduce heat and add salsa and tomatoes. Simmer 1 minute and spoon over tortillas. Top with cheese and a dollop of low-fat sour cream, if desired.

**Vegetarian. Serves 3.**

# Where's-the-Tuna & Noodles Casserole

Really easy!

8 ounces whole-wheat noodles, cooked and drained

1 package frozen mixed vegetables

1 can low-sodium, low-fat mushroom soup

1 cup low-fat mozzarella or soy cheese, shredded

1 recipe Where's-the-Tuna Salad, page 61

Wheat germ

Preheat oven to 350 degrees. Mix all ingredients except the "tuna" salad and wheat germ. Pour into a nonstick baking pan and place spoonfuls of salad throughout the noodle mix. Top with wheat germ. Bake for 20 minutes until bubbly.

**Vegetarian. Serves 2–3.**

## Pasta with Black Bean & Tomato Sauce

Slightly spicy, this is great for a change of pace from the usual spaghetti sauce. It's really good with fruit salad and our Corn Bread from Emily, page 49.

1 tablespoon olive oil

2 cloves garlic, minced

1 teaspoon chili powder

1 teaspoon ground cumin

1 can (14.5 ounces) stewed tomatoes

1 can (15 ounces) black beans, drained and rinsed

12 ounces whole-wheat pasta

In a large nonstick skillet, heat oil over medium heat. Add garlic and cook for 1 minute, stirring frequently. Add chili powder and cumin, and cook for 1 additional minute. Add tomatoes and beans; break up tomatoes while stirring. When sauce just begins to boil, cover, reduce heat to low, and simmer 20 minutes. Cook pasta according to package directions and drain. Serve sauce over pasta.

**Vegan. Serves 4.**

## Peanutty Peas & Noodles

Be sure you save the leftovers of this noodle dish. It tastes great cold and makes an easy-to-pack lunch.

8 ounces whole-wheat spaghetti

1/3 cup natural peanut butter

1/2 cup hot water

1 tablespoon rice vinegar

2 tablespoons safflower oil

1 teaspoon reduced-sodium soy sauce

1 teaspoon lemon juice

Dash garlic powder

1/2 cup frozen peas, thawed (or substitute your child's favorite vegetable)

Cook spaghetti according to package directions. While spaghetti is cooking, combine peanut butter and hot water in a small bowl. Whisk until smooth. Add remaining ingredients, except peas, and stir well. Toss spaghetti with peanut butter sauce, add peas, and serve.

**Vegan. Serves 3.**

# No-Noodle Lasagna

Oh, those bags of mixed frozen vegetables—such a blessing for the busy parent! Don't feel too guilty about not using fresh veggies; frozen vegetables retain many nutrients, have zero fat, and are usually very acceptable to kids' taste buds. Tofu takes the place of the noodles in this lasagna.

1 jar (14.5 ounces) low-fat spaghetti sauce

1 package (10.5 ounces) tofu, extra firm, drained and thinly sliced

1 package (16 ounces) mixed frozen broccoli, green beans, onions, and red peppers, thawed and drained

1 cup low-fat ricotta cheese

1/4 cup Parmesan cheese, grated

1/2 cup low-fat cheddar or mozzarella cheese, shredded

In a large nonstick skillet, heat 1 cup spaghetti sauce over low to medium heat. Add half the tofu slices in a layer over the sauce. Cover tofu with vegetables. In a small bowl, combine ricotta and Parmesan cheeses. Gently spread cheese mixture over vegetables. Top with remaining tofu slices and spaghetti sauce. Cover and cook over low heat for 15 minutes until mixture is heated through. Remove from heat. Sprinkle with cheddar or mozzarella cheese and let stand for 2 minutes.

**Vegetarian. Serves 4.**

# Bulgur Wheat & Veggies

A great variation from rice or pasta, bulgur wheat will surely become a staple in your kitchen.

1 cup bulgur wheat

2 cups water

Juice of 1 lemon

1 tablespoon dill weed

1 cup carrots, sliced

1 cup peas

1/8 cup reduced-sodium soy sauce

1/4 cup water

1 teaspoon garlic powder

In a small saucepan, combine bulgur and water. Cover. Bring to a boil over medium heat. Cook until water is fully absorbed and bulgur is fluffy (about 15 minutes). Add the lemon juice and dill to the bulgur. Set aside. In a small skillet, cook carrots and peas in soy sauce, water, and garlic powder 5 minutes over medium to high heat. Pour over bulgur wheat.

**Vegan. Serves 4.**

# Simple Goulash

No one will know there's no meat in this tasty meal. Serve with sliced apples or pears, and a crusty whole-grain bread.

1 green pepper, chopped

1 onion, chopped

2 2/3 cups meat substitute
  (such as crumbled veggie burgers)

2 cans (15 ounces each) tomato sauce

Salt and pepper to taste

4 cups star-shaped pasta, cooked

In a large saucepan sprayed with vegetable cooking spray, sauté green pepper and onion. Add meat substitute and tomato sauce. Heat through. Add salt and pepper to taste. Serve over cooked pasta.

**Vegetarian. Serves 8.**

# Greek Spaghetti

This is so simple and so good! It makes a great meal served with a Greek salad.

1 package (12-ounces) whole-wheat
  noodles, cooked and drained

1/2 cup sliced pitless black olives

1/2 cup crumbled feta cheese, plus extra
  for topping

1 can (8 ounces) sliced, unmarinated
  artichoke hearts

Mix warm, cooked noodles with the olives, feta cheese, and artichoke hearts. Serve warm. Crumble a bit of feta cheese on top.

**Vegetarian. Serves 4.**

# Veggie Stew

Here's a quick-cooking stew that's guaranteed to be a kid-pleaser—we think it's "veggie, veggie good!" If you cook it longer, it's even better.

1 tablespoon safflower oil

2 tablespoons vegetable broth
  (canned or made from a bouillon cube)

1/2 clove garlic, chopped

3 carrots, thinly sliced

1 large zucchini, thinly sliced

1 onion, thinly sliced

1 can (15 ounces) chickpeas, drained and
  rinsed

1 can (14.5 ounces) stewed tomatoes

Dash pepper

2 cups cooked whole-wheat couscous
  (or other whole-grain or pasta)

In a large nonstick skillet, heat oil and broth over medium heat. Add garlic, carrots, zucchini, and onion. Sauté about 10 minutes or until tender. Add chickpeas, tomatoes, and pepper. Lower heat and simmer 15 minutes. Serve over hot couscous.

**Vegan. Serves 4.**

# Mediterranean "Chicken"

Very easy, serve this quick dinner with a field greens salad with a light balsamic vinegar and olive oil dressing, and a green vegetable such as fresh lima beans or fresh broccoli (see Joey & Michael's "Trees," page 108).

1 1/2 cups bulgur wheat

1 can (16 ounces) stewed tomatoes, chopped

1 can vegetable stock

1/2 soup can of water

1 tablespoon lemon juice

Wheat germ

2 meatless "chicken" breasts

**Optional:**

Sliced black olives

Chopped parsley

Paprika

Preheat oven to 350 degrees. Mix all ingredients except the "chicken" pieces. Pour into a nonstick baking dish. Place "chicken" on top, pressing down into the bulgur wheat mixture. Sprinkle with wheat germ. Optional: sprinkle with sliced black olives, chopped parsley, and paprika for a bit more spice. Cover with foil and bake for 30 minutes. Remove foil and bake another 10 minutes.

**Vegetarian. Serves 2–3.**

# Meatless Meat Loaf

This is made just like you would make it with real ground beef. It's a little less likely to "stick" together, so you may want to use an extra beaten egg to bind it more. It's easy, delicious, and nutritious!

1 package ground meat substitute

1/2 cup bread crumbs (you may add more if you use an extra egg)

1 egg, beaten

1/4 onion, chopped

2 stalks celery, chopped

1 firm tomato, chopped finely

1 can (16 ounces) tomato paste

1/4 cup pumpkin seeds, unsalted

cheese of your choice, shredded

Preheat oven to 350 degrees. Mix all ingredients, except cheese, well and shape into a loaf. Place in a nonstick loaf pan and bake 30–40 minutes. Let cool for a few minutes, sprinkle with shredded cheese, and serve with brown rice or couscous, and a salad.

**Vegetarian. Serves 4–5.**

## Tofu Tenders

This vegetarian version of chicken or fish sticks will please kids of all ages. Serve with catsup, mustard, or salad dressing for dipping.

3/4 cup wheat germ

Dash of salt-free, all-purpose seasoning

1/2 teaspoon chili powder

1 package (10.5 ounces) tofu, extra firm, drained

1/4 cup soy milk

Preheat oven to 375 degrees. Combine wheat germ, seasoning, and chili powder in a shallow bowl, and mix well. Spray a large wire rack or baking sheet with vegetable spray. Cut tofu into about 20 sticks, approximately 1/2 inch wide. Dip each stick in milk, roll it in the wheat germ mixture, and place on wire rack. Bake for 35 minutes, or until crisp and brown.

**Vegan. Serves 3.**

## Baked Vegetables

This dish is for nights when you have a little more time, and it's worth the wait. The baking root vegetables will fill your kitchen with a rich aroma that says, "There's no place like home."

2 medium potatoes, peeled and cut into 1-inch pieces

2 medium carrots, peeled and cut into 1/2-inch slices

1 tablespoon olive oil

1 teaspoon each basil and oregano

1/4 teaspoon each salt and freshly ground black pepper

1 large zucchini, cut into 1/2-inch pieces

1 large red bell pepper, cut into 1-inch pieces

2 cloves garlic, minced

Preheat oven to 425 degrees. Place potatoes and carrots in 9 x 13–inch baking pan sprayed with vegetable cooking spray. Drizzle with oil; sprinkle with basil, oregano, salt, and pepper. Toss lightly to coat. Bake 20 minutes. Add zucchini, red pepper, and garlic; stir into potato-carrot mixture. Return to oven and bake 20 minutes more or until vegetables are tender.

**Vegan. Serves 4.**

**Better than** peanut butter & jelly

# Stuffed Eggplant

This recipe is a wonderful way to introduce your child to eggplant. Serve with stewed tomatoes, brown rice, and a salad of greens for a complete meal.

2 medium eggplants

1/2 onion, chopped

1 1/2 cups low-fat cheddar cheese, grated

1 tablespoon parsley, chopped

1 egg or equivalent Egg Replacer

1/2 cup unsalted sunflower seeds

4 tablespoons bread crumbs or wheat germ

Preheat oven to 400 degrees. Wash eggplants and trim stem ends. Place eggplants in a large saucepan. Add water to cover. Bring to boil and cook until eggplants are just barely tender when pierced with a knife, about 5 minutes. Drain and cool. Cut eggplants in half lengthwise. Scoop out pulp, leaving a 1/4-inch shell. Mash pulp and set aside. Spray a large baking dish with vegetable cooking spray. Place eggplant shells, skin-side down, in baking dish. Mix all other ingredients except bread crumbs with mashed eggplant. Spoon mixture into eggplant shells. Top with bread crumbs. Bake for 20–30 minutes or until golden brown.

**Vegetarian. Serves 4.**

# Stuffed Green Peppers

This recipe takes about an hour from start to finish, but much of that is baking time, allowing you freedom to join in other family activities.

4 large green peppers, cut in half lengthwise

3/4 cup onion, chopped

1/2 pound fresh mushrooms, chopped

2 tablespoons canola oil

1 cup cooked brown rice

3 tablespoons mild green chilies, chopped

2 eggs, slightly beaten

1 cup vegetable broth, canned or made from a vegetable bouillon cube

Preheat oven to 350 degrees. In a saucepan, parboil peppers for about 5 minutes or until slightly done. Drain and set aside. In a nonstick saucepan, sauté onions and mushrooms in canola oil until just barely cooked. Stir in rice and green chilies. Remove from heat and mix with eggs. Stuff each pepper half with rice mixture and place in a baking dish sprayed with vegetable cooking spray. Pour vegetable broth in bottom of dish. Bake peppers for 45 minutes, basting 2 or 3 times with the hot broth. When peppers are tender but not falling apart, transfer them to a serving dish. Pour baking liquid over peppers and serve.

**Vegetarian. Serves 4.**

## Taco-less Taco Salad

Even though there are no taco shells or chips in this recipe, it tastes as authentic as any more traditional version.

2 cups meat substitute, crumbled

1 can (15.5 ounces) kidney beans, drained and rinsed

1 jar (8 ounces) taco sauce

1 clove garlic, minced

2 cups iceberg or romaine lettuce, shredded

1 cup green pepper, chopped

4 tomatoes, chopped

2 cups low-fat cheddar cheese, shredded

In a medium saucepan, combine meat substitute with beans, taco sauce, and garlic. Heat 3–4 minutes. Serve on plates starting with a layer of shredded lettuce, then green pepper, tomatoes, then the "meat" mixture topped with cheddar cheese.

**Vegetarian. Serves 6.**

## Couscous Tacos

Serve with soy chips and guacamole for a real south-of-the-border flavor.

1 can (14.5 ounces) Mexican-style stewed tomatoes

1 cup red kidney beans, drained and rinsed

3/4 cup vegetable broth or water

1/3 cup onion, chopped

4 teaspoons taco seasoning mix

1 cup whole-wheat or regular uncooked couscous

1 package (10.5 ounces) tofu, extra firm, drained and crumbled

8 taco shells, heated

1 cup lettuce, chopped

1 cup low-fat cheddar cheese, shredded

Salsa

Low-fat sour cream

In a large saucepan over medium heat, combine undrained stewed tomatoes, beans, vegetable broth, onion, and taco seasoning. Bring to a boil. Stir in couscous and tofu. Cover and remove from stove. Let stand 5 minutes. Spoon couscous mixture into taco shells. Top with lettuce, cheese, salsa, and sour cream.

**Vegetarian. Serves 4.**

**Better than** peanut butter & jelly

# Cheesy "Chicken" Enchiladas

Homemade Mexican meals can be a lot healthier than eating out, since you control the amount and type of ingredients, plus, you can use whole-grain products. Very few Mexican restaurants do!

1 cup cheddar cheese, shredded, plus extra for topping

1/2 cup cow, soy, or rice milk

Dash chili powder (optional)

1 can (8 ounces) chopped green chilies, mild

8 whole-wheat flour tortillas

1 package meatless "chicken breasts," cut into small pieces

1 cup salsa

Preheat oven to 350 degrees. Mix cheese, milk, chili powder and green chilies. Spread over tortillas and add pieces of "chicken breasts." Roll up and lay tightly in baking dish. Cover with salsa and more shredded cheese. Bake for 25 minutes until hot and bubbly. Serve with brown rice, fresh green salad, and guacamole.

**Vegetarian. Serves 4.**

# Too-Tired Tortillas

Fix this when you are too tired to fuss over dinner. It'll get you through those mid-week "hump" days before you can start counting down to the weekend!

1 can (16 ounces) vegetarian refried beans

1 jar (11 ounces) salsa

4 large whole-wheat tortillas

1 cup cheddar cheese, grated, plus extra for topping

**Optional toppings:**

  low-fat yogurt

  prepared guacamole

  **minced green onions**

In a small saucepan, warm beans and three-quarters of the salsa over medium heat for 5 minutes. Meanwhile, place tortillas on a microwave-safe plate, and cover with a damp paper towel. Heat on high 20–30 seconds or until warm. (You can also heat tortillas in a 350-degree oven by stacking them, up to 10 at a time, and wrapping in aluminum foil. Heat through for about 10 minutes.)

Spread a quarter of the bean mixture in center of each tortilla. Top with 1/4 cup grated cheese. Roll up tortillas. Serve with remaining salsa, low-fat yogurt, guacamole, chopped green onions, or extra cheese.

**Vegetarian. Serves 4.**

# Fried Rice

Cook up a large batch of brown rice on the weekend and use it for recipes like this during the week.

2 tablespoons canola oil

1/4 cup onion, diced

1/4 cup green pepper, diced

1/4 cup celery, diced

2 cups cooked brown rice

1/2 cup cooked peas

2 eggs, beaten slightly

1/4 cup bean sprouts

Tamari sauce, low sodium

In a large nonstick skillet, heat oil over medium-high heat. Add onions, green pepper, and celery. Sauté until just tender. Remove from skillet and set aside. Add rice to skillet and sauté for 1 minute. Push to the edges, forming a ring of rice around a cleared area of the skillet, and drop the eggs in. Cook them as you would scrambled eggs, leaving the rice ring untouched. Once cooked, mix with rice and return the cooked vegetables to skillet. Add peas. Stir-fry for 2–3 minutes. Add bean sprouts and stir. Season with tamari sauce to taste.

**Vegetarian. Serves 4.**

# Sweet & Sour Tofu

We've substituted tofu for the red-dyed pork that's usually found in this dish. This reduces the fat content of the recipe considerably. The familiar "sweet and sour" taste is still there, although a bit more delicate.

1 can (16 ounces) pineapple chunks (packed in juice), drained; reserve 1 cup juice

1/4 cup reduced-sodium soy sauce

1/4 cup vinegar

1 large tomato cut into wedges

2 1/2 tablespoons cornstarch dissolved in 1/4 cup vegetable broth or water

1 teaspoon ground ginger

1 package (10.5 ounces) tofu, extra firm, drained

2 tablespoons sesame oil

1 green pepper, thinly sliced

1 red pepper, thinly sliced

2 carrots, thinly sliced

2 cups brown rice, cooked

In a small bowl, mix pineapple juice, soy sauce, vinegar, tomato, cornstarch mixture, and ginger. Slice tofu into 1-inch cubes. In a large nonstick skillet, heat oil over low to medium heat. Stir-fry tofu 10 minutes. Add peppers and carrots, and stir-fry 3 more minutes. Stir soy sauce mixture; add to skillet. Cook, stirring constantly, until sauce thickens, about 5 minutes. Add drained pineapple chunks and heat through. Serve over hot rice.

**Vegan. Serves 4.**

## Beans & "Franks"

If you've never tried meatless hot dogs before, you and your kids are in for a pleasant and healthy surprise. Most brands are made from soy protein, have little or no fat, and are free of nitrates. They even look and taste (almost) like the real thing. They're great in this recipe or served in time-honored fashion on a toasted hot dog roll with mustard and relish.

1 clove garlic, minced

1 tablespoon catsup

2 cans (16 ounces each) vegetarian baked beans

1 package tofu "hot dogs"

3 slices low-fat cheddar cheese, cut into strips

Preheat oven to 350 degrees. Spray an 8-inch square baking pan or casserole dish with vegetable cooking spray. Combine garlic and catsup with beans, and pour into prepared pan. Cut "hot dogs" into bite-size pieces and gently place in bean mixture. Arrange cheese strips in a pattern over the top. Bake, uncovered, 20–30 minutes.

**Vegetarian. Serves 6.**

## Vegetable Risotto

The vegetable contents can vary, especially in the summer when there's a choice of lots of fresh veggies.

1 tablespoon olive oil

1 onion, chopped

1/2 cup carrots, chopped

1 cup frozen or fresh peas

1 cup mushrooms, chopped

1 cup brown long-grain rice, uncooked

2 1/2 cups vegetable broth, canned or made from vegetable bouillon cubes

1 tablespoon tomato paste

1 teaspoon dried mixed herbs

Salt and pepper

1 small can (8 ounces) sweet corn

In a large nonstick skillet, heat oil over medium heat. Add onion and sauté 3 minutes. Add carrots, peas, mushrooms, and rice, and cook 2 more minutes, stirring constantly. Add broth, tomato paste, herbs, and seasonings to taste. Bring to a boil. Cover, reduce heat, and simmer for 45 minutes. Add corn, re-cover, and cook 5 minutes.

**Vegan. Serves 4.**

# Spaghetti Squash Spaghetti

Your kids are bound to enjoy these new "noodles"! They are surprisingly pasta-like, although they do taste like squash. Like regular pasta, they should be cooked just until the "al dente" stage, or they become mushy and limp. You can usually find low-fat marinara sauce in the natural food section of your grocery store. If you can't, then check labels for sauce with the lowest fat content.

1 medium spaghetti squash
2 cups low-fat marinara sauce
Parmesan cheese, grated

Preheat oven to 350 degrees. Slice squash in half lengthwise and remove seeds. Bake cut-side down until tender when pierced with fork, or about 50–60 minutes. Use a fork to pull the "spaghetti" strands out of the squash. Place in bowl. Heat marinara sauce and pour over strands. Top with Parmesan cheese.

**Vegetarian. Serves 4.**

# Veggie Kabobs

So good and elegant they can even be a company dinner. We broil these kabobs in the oven, but they can also be cooked over a charcoal grill. We often bring them to share at summer cookouts hosted by nonvegetarian friends. Now people ask for them! **Note:** Only adults should handle skewers.

Cut each into a total of 8 pieces:
   1 medium onion
   1 medium red pepper
   1 medium green pepper
   1 medium zucchini squash
   2 ears cooked corn
12 large mushrooms
8 cherry tomatoes
1/2 cup olive oil
red-wine or balsamic vinegar
1 clove garlic, crushed
Salt and pepper to taste

Evenly distribute vegetable pieces in a pleasing pattern among skewers. In a small bowl, mix olive oil, vinegar, garlic, salt, and pepper. Brush on vegetables until well coated. Place skewered vegetables on a broiling pan and grill under a preheated broiler on each side until done, about 10–12 minutes each side. Remove from skewers. Serve over cooked rice or couscous.

**Vegan. Makes 4 generous portions.**

# Veggie Pie

This is one of our favorite recipes. It's worth the effort and introduces your children to some wonderful flavors.

2 cups cooked wild rice

4 tablespoons tahini

4 tablespoons sesame seeds, toasted

4 tablespoons whole-wheat flour

1 cup cooked spinach, chopped

1/2 cup cooked carrots, sliced

1 cup low-fat ricotta cheese

2 eggs, beaten

4 tablespoons Parmesan cheese, grated

Preheat oven to 350 degrees. Spray an 8-inch glass pie plate with vegetable cooking spray. In a large bowl, combine rice, tahini, sesame seeds, and flour. Press mixture into pie plate. Layer first spinach, then carrots over rice crust. Combine ricotta and beaten eggs, and pour over top layer. Sprinkle with Parmesan and bake, uncovered, for 20 minutes until heated through and lightly browned.

**Vegetarian. Serves 4.**

# Chili Your Way

Use your imagination and add or change ingredients creatively. We also mix up the kinds of beans we use. Each time we make this, it's different!

1 can (15.5 ounces) red kidney beans, drained and rinsed

1 can (15 ounces) chickpeas, drained and rinsed

1 can (15 ounces) white kidney beans, drained and rinsed

3 cans (14.5 ounces each) stewed tomatoes

1 zucchini, sliced

1 sweet potato, peeled and diced

2 carrots, peeled and sliced

1 small can (8 ounces) corn, drained

2 tablespoons chili powder

1 clove garlic, crushed

1/4 cup parsley, chopped

1 tablespoon cilantro, chopped

Dash each of cumin and red pepper flakes

4 cups cooked brown rice (optional)

Sauté zucchini, carrots, and sweet potato until crisp-tender in a saucepan coated with vegetable cooking spray. Combine beans and stewed tomatoes in a large pot and add sautéed vegetables. Add seasonings and cook slowly for 45 minutes to 1 hour. Serve over rice, if desired.

**Vegan. Serves 8.**

## Okra Casserole
## for Busy People

Okra, often used in Creole dishes like gumbo, has a flavor reminiscent of eggplant. Fresh okra is more flavorful and nutritious than canned but is also harder to find unless you live in the southern United States. This is a great backup recipe for when the cupboard seems bare!

1 can (14.5 ounces) okra, drained

1/2 cup brown rice, uncooked

1 cup water

1/2 cup mild green chilies, chopped

1 cup tomato sauce

Preheat oven to 350 degrees. In a medium saucepan, place okra, rice, water, and green chilies. Cover and bring to a boil. Reduce heat to low and simmer 40 minutes or until rice is tender. Stir in tomato sauce. Spray 8-inch square baking pan with vegetable cooking spray. Pour mixture into pan. Bake uncovered for 10 minutes.

**Vegan. Serves 4.**

## Spinach Casserole
## They'll Really Like

No kidding—you won't hear complaints about spinach anymore. We were surprised at reactions to this casserole, especially when we ran out!

2 cups cooked brown rice

1 cup low-fat cheddar cheese, grated

4 eggs, beaten

2 tablespoons fresh parsley, chopped

1 package (10 ounces) frozen chopped spinach, thawed and drained

1 tablespoon canola oil

4 tablespoons wheat germ

Preheat oven to 350 degrees. Combine the cooked rice and cheese. Add eggs and parsley. Stir in the drained chopped spinach. Spray a casserole dish with vegetable cooking spray. Add mixture to casserole dish. In a small bowl, combine wheat germ and canola oil. Top casserole with wheat germ mixture. Bake, uncovered, for 40 minutes.

**Vegetarian. Serves 4.**

**Better than** peanut butter & jelly

# Chickpea & Spinach Casserole

For speed and convenience, we use frozen spinach in this recipe, but if you have time, washed and finely chopped fresh spinach is even more nutritious.

1 tablespoon olive oil

1 medium onion, diced

1 garlic clove, minced

1 package (10 ounces) frozen spinach, thawed and drained

1 1/2 cups tomato sauce

1 can (15 ounces) chickpeas, drained and rinsed

Salt and pepper to taste

1/2 cup low-fat Monterey Jack cheese, grated

1/2 cup wheat germ

3 cups whole-wheat couscous, cooked

Preheat oven to 350 degrees. In a large non-stick skillet, heat oil over medium heat. Add onion and sauté 5–6 minutes. Add garlic and cook 1 minute more, stirring constantly. Add spinach and mix well. Fold in tomato sauce and chickpeas. Remove from heat. Season with salt and pepper. Spray an 8-inch square or 9-inch round baking dish with vegetable cooking spray. Add chickpea mixture. Top with grated cheese and wheat germ. Bake 15–20 minutes. Serve over couscous.

**Vegetarian. Serves 6.**

# Eggplant & Pasta Casserole

Excellent served with fresh, cooked broccoli and sliced tomatoes or a green salad.

1 large eggplant, peeled and sliced into 1/2-inch rounds

Olive oil

2 cups low-fat marinara sauce

1/2 cup grated Parmesan cheese

1/4 cup unsalted sunflower seeds

12 ounces whole-wheat pasta, cooked and drained

1 1/2 cups mozzarella cheese, grated or sliced

Preheat broiler. Brush eggplant slices with olive oil. Place on broiling pan and broil until lightly browned and tender on both sides. Turn frequently. Remove from oven and set aside. Decrease oven temperature to 350 degrees. In a blender or food processor, blend the marinara sauce, Parmesan cheese, and sunflower seeds until smooth.

Spray rectangular baking pan with vegetable cooking spray. Place pasta on bottom of pan. Add eggplant. Top with sauce mixture. Sprinkle with mozzarella cheese. Bake 30 minutes, uncovered, until bubbly and hot.

**Vegetarian. Serves 4.**

# Vegetarian Spaghetti Sauce

Make extra batches of this sauce for use in other recipes. Frozen, it will keep for up to three months.

2 tablespoons olive oil

2 cups zucchini, cut into matchstick-size pieces

1/2 cup mushrooms, sliced

1/2 cup green pepper, chopped

1/2 cup onion, chopped

1/2 teaspoon garlic powder

1 can (14.5 ounces) stewed tomatoes, cut up

1 small can (6 ounces) tomato paste

1/2 cup water

1 teaspoon salt

1/2 teaspoon pepper

1 tablespoon fresh parsley, chopped

1 teaspoon oregano

In a large nonstick skillet, heat oil over medium heat. Add vegetables (except tomatoes) and garlic powder. Sauté 3 minutes or until tender. Add tomatoes, tomato paste, water, and seasonings. Bring just to a boil. Lower heat and simmer, uncovered, for 20 minutes. Stir frequently. Serve over cooked spaghetti.

**Vegan. Serves 6.**

# Stuffed Zucchini

This dish will make zucchini lovers out of your family. Serve with brown rice or quinoa pasta and a fruit salad.

4 medium zucchini sliced lengthwise

3 tablespoons olive oil

3/4 medium onion, minced

3 cloves fresh garlic, crushed

Salt and pepper

1/4 cup walnuts, crushed

1 1/2 tablespoons flour

1/2 cup feta cheese, crumbled

3/4 cup Swiss cheese, grated

2 tablespoons fresh parsley, chopped

1 tablespoon fresh dill, chopped

3 beaten eggs

Wheat germ

Paprika

Preheat oven to 375 degrees. Scoop out insides of zucchini, leaving a 1/2-inch rim. Chop the scooped zucchini into small bits and sauté in olive oil with onions, garlic, salt and pepper until soft. Combine cooked onions with walnuts, flour, cheeses, herbs, and beaten eggs. Fill zucchini shells; top with wheat germ and paprika. Place in a baking pan and bake for 30 minutes.

**Vegetarian. Serves 4**

Better than peanut butter & jelly

## Portabella Mushroom "Steak" Dinner

These giant, tasty mushrooms are now available almost everywhere, and even nonvegetarian restaurants may offer them as a burger or steak alternative.

2 tablespoons olive oil

1 garlic clove, chopped

6 large portabella mushrooms, sliced

1 teaspoon tamari sauce

6 pieces of whole-wheat toast

1/4 cup Parmesan cheese, grated

In a large nonstick skillet, heat oil over medium heat. Add garlic and sauté for 2–3 minutes. Add mushrooms and tamari sauce and sauté until mushrooms are just done, about 5–7 minutes. Top each toast slice with an even serving of mushrooms. Sprinkle with Parmesan cheese.

**Vegetarian. Serves 6.**

## Pepper "Steak"

This vegetarian version is every bit as good as the original meat-based recipe.

1 green pepper, seeded and coarsely chopped

1/2 onion, coarsely chopped

1 tablespoon olive oil

1 package meatless beef-substitute strips

1 tomato, sliced thinly

2 tablespoons stir-fry sauce—use your favorite brand

2 cups cooked brown rice

In a medium stir-fry pan over medium-hot heat, stir-fry peppers and onions in the oil until just crisp. Add "beef" strips, tomato, and stir-fry sauce and cook, stirring for 2 minutes. Add more stir-fry sauce if needed. Serve over brown rice.

**Vegetarian. Serves 2–3.**

# Arnie's Pizzas

Marty's husband created these veggie pizzas. Both variations are fast and nutritious.

1 large pizza crust

1 can (6 ounces) tomato paste

1 package (8 ounces) low-fat mozzarella cheese, shredded

## Topping 1:

8 fresh mushrooms, sliced

1 small zucchini, sliced

2 green onions, sliced

1 medium tomato, sliced

## Topping 2:

8 fresh mushrooms, sliced

1 package (4 ounces) feta cheese, crumbled

1 cup broccoli florets, cut small

1 medium tomato, sliced

Preheat oven to 375 degrees. Spread tomato paste and mozzarella cheese over pizza crust and add your choice of toppings. Bake for 20 minutes or until crust browns and cheese is bubbly.

**Vegetarian. Serves 4.**

# Zucchini Pizza

This pizza uses fresh tomato, not canned paste or sauce, as its base.

1 pizza crust (or focaccia bread round)

3/4 cup low-fat ricotta cheese

2 tablespoons fresh basil leaves, chopped

1/4 teaspoon salt

1/8 teaspoon pepper

1 large tomato, very thinly sliced

1 medium zucchini, very thinly sliced lengthwise

2 tablespoons Parmesan cheese, grated (optional)

1 teaspoon olive oil

Preheat oven to 375 degrees. Place pizza crust on baking sheet and heat for 5 minutes. In the meantime, combine ricotta cheese, basil leaves, salt, and pepper; set aside. Remove partially cooked crust from oven, top with tomato slices, then top with ricotta mixture. Arrange sliced zucchini on top and sprinkle with Parmesan; drizzle with oil. Using a pancake turner, slide pizza off baking sheet and place directly on oven rack. Bake 8 to 10 minutes, or until dough is crisp and cheese is melted. To serve, cut into 8 slices.

**Vegetarian. Serves 4.**

# nutrition-packed
# **Snacks**

Snacks can be an excellent way for young children to consume some of the calories they need each day—as long as the snacks are nutritious. It's hard to compete with the cleverly packaged, high-fat, and sugary snacks kids see on TV and in the supermarket. But if you are a little creative, you can get your children excited about fresh fruit, veggies, or other wholesome foods for snacks. Use your imagination in offering either fresh or precooked items. Even cooked, cold brown rice topped with reduced-sodium soy or tamari sauce makes a wonderful snack.

If they're ready for it, let your children take some responsibility for what they snack on by keeping a pantry shelf they can reach stocked with items you approve of, such as pretzels, rice cakes, or mini-boxes of raisins.

## Super-Quick Snacks

Dried fruits (try bananas, mango slices, or pineapple spears) and fruit roll-ups (made from only fruit).

Low-fat, plain yogurt combined with fresh fruit, sunflower seeds, or raisins.

Whole fresh strawberries, frozen, for an instant fruit dessert or snack.

Fresh vegetables sliced into "sticks." Try zucchini, carrots, red or green peppers, celery, green beans, radishes, or even raw organic potatoes!

Easy-to-eat fruit, such as grapes, grape-fruit, apples, oranges, and bananas. Be sure to cut fruit into small pieces—especially the grapes, as whole grapes can be a chok-ing hazard to children under five years old.

Popcorn, air-popped or microwaved. (Be sure to purchase a brand that has no added salt, dyes, or sugar.) Popcorn is not for kids under five—it is a choking hazard.

Graham crackers, rice cakes, mini-bagels, and unsalted pretzels.

## Mango Madness Shake

Smooth and satisfying.

6–8 ice cubes
1 cup mango chunks, peeled
1 cup low-fat yogurt, vanilla or plain
1/2 cup soy milk

In a food processor or blender, crush ice cubes. Add remaining ingredients and blend until smooth.

**Vegetarian. Serves 4.**

## Apple Dips

Another wonderful use for natural peanut butter.

1 apple, peeled and cut into slices
1/4 cup natural peanut butter
1/4 cup wheat germ

Top apple slices with peanut butter, then dip in wheat germ.

**Vegan. Serves 2.**

# Trail Mix

Drop a small handful of this nutritious mix in a plastic baggie and your child can munch her way through a "boring" car ride or shopping trip. Also great as a movie snack.

1/4 cup dried banana chips

3/4 cup Corn Chex

1/2 cup dried apples

1/4 cup raisins

1/4 cup unsalted peanuts

1/4 cup sunflower seeds

1/4 cup low-fat granola

1/4 cup unsalted mini-pretzels

1/4 cup carob chips

In a large bowl, combine all ingredients and mix well. Store in an air-tight container and keep in a cool place. Stays fresh for two weeks.

**Vegan. Makes 3 cups.**

# Chewies for Charlie

Charlie is a Labrador retriever who, as a puppy, would eat anything. This recipe met the challenge, "Let's see if Charlie likes peanut butter." He did, and after tasting this snack, so did everyone else! These "chewies" make a great packable snack. They keep nicely in the refrigerator for up to 4 days.

1/4 cup low-fat granola

1 tablespoon maple syrup

1/4 cup sunflower seeds

1/4 cup raisins

1/4 cup carrots, finely shredded

1 tablespoon wheat germ

3/4 cup natural peanut butter

In a small bowl, combine granola, maple syrup, sunflower seeds, raisins, carrots, and wheat germ. Blend in peanut butter. Form into small balls.

**Vegan. Serves 10.**

## Cucumber Snacks

The sunflower seeds add a nice crunch to this quick and easy snack.

2 celery stalks, trimmed and cut in chunks

1 large carrot, peeled and cut in chunks

1/4 cup sunflower seeds

1/4 cup low-fat yogurt, plain

2 tablespoons soy mayonnaise

1 cucumber

In a food processor or blender, blend celery and carrots until finely chopped. Transfer to a bowl. In food processor or blender, combine seeds, yogurt, and mayonnaise. Blend thoroughly. Add to carrot and celery mixture. Peel cucumber and slice lengthwise. Remove seeds and fill cavity with mixture. Serve chilled.

**Vegetarian. Serves 2.**

## Fruit Refresher Shake

This cool fruit shake is appropriate anytime.

4 ripe bananas, peeled

12 strawberries

4 cups orange juice

4 cups seltzer water

Put all ingredients in a food processor or blender and blend for about 2 minutes. Chill well and serve. Top with fresh blueberries, if desired.

**Vegan. Serves 6–8.**

## Banana Berry Blast

This nutritious shake is a great source of calcium when you use enriched soy or rice milk. You can use any combination of fresh or frozen fruit.

2–3 ice cubes

1 banana, sliced

1 cup frozen strawberries, no sugar added

1/2 cup soy milk or rice milk

1 tablespoon frozen apple juice concentrate

1 teaspoon wheat germ

In a food processor or blender, crush ice cubes. Add all other ingredients and blend until smooth. Serve immediately.

**Vegan. Serves 2.**

## Roundup Rice Cakes

This snack makes a great lunch, too.

8 pitted dates, chopped

4 ounces low-fat cream cheese

1/8 teaspoon ginger, grated

1/2 cup walnuts, chopped

1/4 cup low-fat cottage cheese

4 rice cakes

1 fresh peach, cut into slices (or canned
   peaches packed in unsweetened juice)

In a small bowl, combine dates and cream
cheese. Add ginger and nuts. Stir until
blended. Add cottage cheese. Mash with a
fork. Divide mixture into fourths and spread
evenly over rice cakes. Top each rice cake
with peach slices.

**Vegetarian. Serves 4.**

## Fizzy Brew

This fizzy punch is perfect for summer
barbeques.

1 bottle (24 ounces) cranberry juice

1 bottle (16 ounces) seltzer water

1 apple, chopped

1 cup red, seedless grapes, quartered

1 lemon peel, peeled in spirals

1 orange peel, peeled in spirals

In a large punch bowl, combine juice and
seltzer with apple and grapes. Add lemon
and orange peels. Chill.

**Vegan. Serves 10.**

## Uncandy Apples

This treat provides a dramatic and delicious change from the way-too-sweet
traditional candied apples.

1/2 cup honey

1/4 cup molasses

1/2 teaspoon lemon juice

4 small apples

Wheat germ to coat

In a small bowl, mix honey and molasses.
Add lemon juice and mix well. Insert a popsicle stick in each apple. Dip apples in honey
mix, then coat with wheat germ.

**Vegetarian. Serves 4.**

## Strawberry-Banana Pops

This is a delicious year-round treat. You can vary the fruit. Be creative!

1 cup frozen low-fat vanilla yogurt or frozen soy dessert

1 cup frozen strawberries

1 banana, sliced

Place all ingredients in a food processor. Blend until smooth. Pour into popsicle holders. Freeze overnight.

**Vegetarian. Serves 4.**

## Apples & Pears

A lovely sit-down snack you could share with your child. The cooking fruit sends a fabulous aroma through the house. This dish freezes well.

3 apples, cored and sliced

2 pears, cored and sliced

1 cup apple juice, unsweetened

1/2 cup raisins

In a medium saucepan, simmer apple and pear slices in apple juice until tender, or about 5–7 minutes. Add raisins and simmer until plump; about 2 minutes. Stir well and serve in bowls.

**Vegan. Serves 4.**

## Popcorn Surprise

Packed with nutrients, this treat looks like the popular and highly sugared caramel-corn snack—but it tastes better! Air-popped popcorn is completely fat-free. We recommend using air-popped popcorn over prepackaged microwave popcorn, which sometimes has a lot of salt, sugar, food dyes, and fake flavorings.

5 cups popped popcorn

1/4 cup peanuts

2 tablespoons sunflower seeds

1 1/2 tablespoons molasses

1/2 cup honey

Preheat oven to 350 degrees. Spray a 9 x 13–inch baking dish with vegetable cooking spray. In a large bowl, combine popcorn, peanuts, and sunflower seeds. In a separate bowl, combine molasses and honey. Stir until well blended. Pour over popcorn mixture. Toss until completely coated. Spread in baking dish or roll into balls and bake for 15 minutes. Remove from oven and let cool.

This snack can be served as a spooky "trick or treat." Arrange popcorn balls in a pot or large cookie jar. Make the top by blowing up a balloon and covering it with a square piece of an old white sheet. Tie a black ribbon around the "neck" to form the ghost's head. Draw a spooky face, and drape your ghost over the serving container.

**Vegetarian. Serves 6–8.**

**Better than** peanut butter & jelly

## Squash Squares

A great way to get both fruit and vegetable food groups into one snack!

1 medium acorn squash

8 bite-sized slices fresh pineapple

1 medium banana, sliced

Bake in 350-degree oven, or in microwave, halved acorn squash with seeds removed. Cool to a comfortable handling temperature and cut into 8 pieces or "squares." Place one slice of pineapple on each square of cooked squash. Top with sliced banana. Serve at room temperature or slightly warm.

**Vegan. Yields 8 snacks.**

## Papaya Fruit Mix

Let your children use their imagination and add or substitute other fruit pieces for color and taste.

1 medium papaya, peeled and sliced into
   2-inch chunks

1 medium banana, sliced

2 tablespoons raisins

Juice of 1 lime

Nutmeg, optional

Mix fruit and lime juice. Top with fresh-ground nutmeg, if desired.

**Vegan. Serves 2.**

## Peanut Butter Tortilla

Small snack-style tortillas are perfect for little hands. Look for them in the refrigerated food section of your grocery store. This filling of peanut butter, honey, and sliced banana tastes wonderful!

1 small-size whole-wheat tortilla

1 tablespoon natural peanut butter

1 teaspoon honey

1 banana, sliced

For each snack, spread whole-wheat tortilla with peanut butter. Drizzle with honey. Top with sliced banana. Roll up.

**Vegetarian. Serves 1.**

## Peanut Butter Nibbles

These little open-face sandwiches will keep a hungry kid going strong.

2 slices whole-grain bread

1/2 cup natural peanut butter

1/2 cup low-fat cream cheese

1 banana, sliced

Spread peanut butter over each bread slice, then add a layer of cream cheese. Top with banana slices. Cut into quarters.

**Vegetarian. Serves 4.**

# Apple Bars

These moist, chewy fruit bars make good additions to school lunches.

1/4 cup raisins

1/4 cup apple juice concentrate, thawed

1/2 cup whole-wheat flour

1/2 cup all-purpose flour

1/2 cup rolled oats

1 tablespoon cinnamon

1 teaspoon baking powder

1 1/4 cups apple, peeled and chopped

2 eggs, whites only

1/2 cup soy milk

1 teaspoon honey or maple syrup

Preheat oven to 350 degrees. Coat an 8-inch square pan with vegetable cooking spray. In a small bowl, combine raisins and apple juice concentrate. Let stand for 20–30 minutes.

Meanwhile, combine flours, oats, cinnamon, and baking powder in a large bowl. Add apple pieces and toss to coat. In a small bowl, combine egg whites, milk, and honey. Pour into flour-apple mixture. Add raisin and juice mixture. Mix gently until evenly moistened (mixture will be thick). Spread into prepared pan. Bake 20 minutes. Remove from oven and let cool. Cut into 2-inch squares.

**Vegetarian. Makes 10–12 bars.**

A parrot.

# Mexican Dip & Chips

Fun food for a crowd, this easy-to-make snack is the perfect thing for an after-school get-together.

1 container (16 ounces) low-fat sour cream

1 packet taco seasoning mix

1 can (16 ounces) vegetarian refried beans

1 jar (11 ounces) salsa

1 cup lettuce, shredded

1 tomato, diced

1 ounce low-fat cheddar cheese, grated

20 ounces natural, low-sodium, low-fat tortilla chips

In a small bowl, combine sour cream and taco seasoning mix. Stir until blended. Spread refried beans on the bottom of a 9 x 13–inch glass pan. Pour sour cream mixture on top. Layer the remaining ingredients in order listed above. Serve with a bowl of tortilla chips.

**Vegetarian. Serves 12–15.**

# scrumptious
# **Desserts**

Desserts and sweets have a place in a child's diet, albeit a small one. As long as a child is eating a variety of healthy foods, we see no harm in serving the occasional dessert—but not as a reward or bribe for eating the main dish!

While we think a total ban on refined sugar is unrealistic, we've chosen to sweeten the following desserts with honey, molasses, and fruit juice instead. Unlike refined sugar, these ingredients have some nutritional value (molasses, for example, is rich in calcium, potassium, chromium, manganese, copper, and zinc). They also add moistness to low-fat and fat-free baked goods, which otherwise tend to be dry. We've also found that desserts made with different sweeteners usually taste better than the usual overpowering sweetness you get with refined sugar.

**Simple Rules-of-Thumb for Dessert Substitutions:**

For sweetening, use fruit juices or applesauce in place of sugar. Unrefined sugar, known as turbinado sugar, may also be used. You'll need to experiment a bit to get the taste the way you want it.

Cut oil, butter, or margarine by half—replace with the same measurement of applesauce or puréed prunes.

Use soy "ice cream" in place of frozen yogurt or regular ice cream.

## Blueberry & Yogurt Crunch

This quick and easy dessert recipe takes just a few minutes to put together but it's so good! Toast the almonds in a hot oven—400 degrees—in a baking pan. Don't use any oil.

1/2 pound fresh blueberries, carefully washed and drained

1 container (8 ounces) plain yogurt

2 tablespoons almond slivers, slightly toasted until caramel brown

Mix blueberries in yogurt. Put toasted, slivered almonds on top. Use fun glasses.

**Vegetarian. Serves 2.**

## Frozen Yogurt Pie

Your kids will enjoy helping you arrange the fruit on top and—even more—helping you eat this delicious dessert!

1 reduced-fat graham cracker crust

1 container (16 ounces) vanilla low-fat frozen yogurt, softened

8 strawberries, sliced

1 cup blueberries

1 ripe peach, pitted and sliced

Scoop frozen yogurt into pie crust. Top with strawberry slices, blueberries, and peach slices. Freeze until ready to serve.

**Vegetarian. Serves 8.**

## Frozen Fruit & Granola Squares

This frozen treat is also good made with crushed strawberries.

1 1/2 cups low-fat granola (or use Make-Your-Own-Granola, page 29)

1 quart low-fat vanilla frozen yogurt, softened

2 cups fresh raspberries, mashed

1 cup strawberry or banana slices (optional)

Spray a 9-inch square pan with vegetable cooking spray. Pour granola evenly over bottom of pan. Spoon yogurt over granola. Spread mashed raspberries over the top, cover, and place in freezer. Freeze about 4 hours or until firm. Cut into squares and top with fresh strawberry or banana slices, if desired.

**Vegetarian. Makes 9–12 servings.**

# Chocolate or Carob Chip Cake

You can use chocolate chips in this recipe, or an equal amount of carob chips, if you want to stay away from chocolate. Carob tastes a lot like chocolate and is often used as a sweetener. It's free of the caffeine in chocolate and is a source of B-vitamins, calcium, and protein. You can find it in chip, powder, or wafer form, sometimes in a regular grocery store but always in your local whole-foods store.

1 1/2 cups all-purpose flour

1/2 cup honey or maple syrup

1 teaspoon baking soda

1/8 teaspoon salt

5 tablespoons vegetable or canola oil

1 teaspoon vanilla

1 tablespoon cider vinegar

1 1/4 cups water

1 cup chocolate or carob chips

Preheat oven to 350 degrees. In a large bowl, combine the flour, honey, baking soda, and salt. Mix well. In a separate bowl, combine oil, vanilla, vinegar, and water. Mix and pour over the dry ingredients. Stir well. Spray an 8 x 8–inch baking pan with vegetable cooking spray. Pour batter into pan. Top with chocolate chips. Bake for 35 minutes or until inserted toothpick comes out clean.

**Vegetarian. Serves 8.**

# Puzzling Pumpkin Pie

No one will ever know there's tofu in this veggie version of the old classic.

1 package (10.5 ounces) tofu, firm, drained

1/3 cup honey or maple syrup

1 cup canned pumpkin

1 teaspoon cinnamon

1/2 teaspoon nutmeg

1/4 teaspoon allspice

Preheat oven to 400 degrees. In a food processor or blender, blend tofu until smooth and creamy. Add honey, pumpkin, and spices; blend well. Pour into a 9-inch unbaked pie shell. Bake 30 minutes or until a toothpick inserted in the center comes out clean. Cool slightly.

**Vegetarian. Serves 8.**

# Brownies to Bedazzle

These delicious brownies have a rich chocolate flavor. Two-year-old Katelyn, one of our "testers," gobbled them up. You can be creative with this brownie recipe and add nuts, sunflower seeds, or wheat germ for added protein. Substitute an equal amount of carob for the chocolate, if you desire.

3 squares unsweetened baking chocolate

6 tablespoons soy milk

3 eggs or equivalent Egg Replacer

3/4 cup honey

1/3 cup maple syrup

1 1/2 teaspoons vanilla

1/2 teaspoon salt

1 cup unbleached white flour

1/4 cup applesauce, unsweetened

Preheat oven to 350 degrees. Spray a 9 x 13–inch baking pan with vegetable cooking spray. Combine chocolate and soy milk in a small saucepan. Cook over very low heat until chocolate is creamy. Remove from heat and let cool. Beat eggs or equivalent with honey, maple syrup, and vanilla. Beat in cooled chocolate and remaining ingredients. Pour into baking pan. Bake for 25 minutes. Cool in pan and cut into squares.

**Vegetarian. Makes 20 squares.**

# Blueberry Cobbler

This healthy version of a traditional dessert has many virtues: it's low in fat, contains no refined sugars, is very easy to prepare, and tastes wonderful!

2/3 cup flour

1 1/2 teaspoons baking powder

1/4 teaspoon salt

1/2 cup soy milk

1/3 cup maple syrup

2 cups blueberries, fresh or frozen

Preheat oven to 350 degrees. In a medium bowl, combine flour, baking powder, and salt. Add soy milk and maple syrup, and whisk until smooth. Lightly spray a casserole dish with vegetable cooking spray. Pour batter into dish and sprinkle blueberries on top. Bake for 40 minutes or until lightly browned.

**Vegan. Serves 6.**

# Apple Crumble

An easy way to fill your house with wonderful baking smells. When family members ask, in anticipation, if you are making an apple pie, you can honestly say, "No, but it's going to be just as good."

4 medium baking apples, peeled and cut into bite-sized pieces

2 tablespoons raisins

2 tablespoons slivered almonds

1/2 teaspoon cinnamon

1/8 teaspoon nutmeg

3/4 cup oats

1/4 cup whole-wheat flour

2 tablespoons oil

1/2 cup apple juice

3 tablespoons maple syrup

Preheat oven to 350 degrees. Spray a 1-quart baking dish with vegetable cooking spray. Add apples, raisins, almonds, cinnamon, and nutmeg to baking dish and mix well. In a separate bowl, combine oats, flour, and oil, and mix until crumbly. Cover apples with crumb mixture. Combine apple juice with maple syrup (may need to heat gently to blend). Pour over crumbs. Bake until apples are tender, 30–40 minutes. Serve warm.

**Vegan. Serves 6.**

# Blue Hawaii Cake

This cake gets its sweetness solely from fruit and fruit juices. It's a guaranteed winner! It's not easy to find a good cake recipe that doesn't use a lot of eggs, sugar, or butter. We treasure this one because it's naturally sweetened and low in fat.

1/4 cup pineapple chunks, fresh or canned

1 egg or equivalent Egg Replacer

1/2 cup unsweetened pineapple juice

1/3 cup orange juice

1 1/2 cups unbleached white flour

1 teaspoon baking soda

1 teaspoon baking powder

1/2 cup fresh blueberries

1/3 cup drained pineapple, crushed

Preheat oven to 350 degrees. Spray an 8-inch square baking pan with vegetable cooking spray. In a large bowl, combine pineapple chunks, egg or equivalent, and pineapple and orange juices. With an electric mixer, beat on medium speed until well blended. Add dry ingredients. Beat well. Gently stir in blueberries and crushed pineapple. Pour batter in pan and smooth evenly. Bake 20–25 minutes until browned and toothpick inserted into center comes out clean.

**Vegetarian. Serves 6.**

# Berry Cake & "Ice Cream"

This is a low-fat version of cake and ice cream, packed with vitamins from fresh fruit!

1 pint fresh strawberries, sliced
1 pint fresh blueberries
1 pint fresh blackberries or raspberries
1 tablespoon maple syrup
1 loaf (1 pound) low-fat pound cake
2 cups low-fat frozen vanilla yogurt
Fresh mint sprigs, optional

In a large bowl, combine all fruit. Add maple syrup; mix well. Let stand about thirty minutes. Slice pound cake into eight slices. Top each slice with a scoop of frozen yogurt, followed by even portions of berry mixture. Top with a sprig of fresh mint, if desired.

**Vegetarian. Serves 8.**

# Banana Cream

This is actually better than ice cream!

2 bananas, thinly sliced
1/2 cup low-fat ricotta cheese
1/4 teaspoon nutmeg
Fresh strawberries or blueberries, sliced

Place sliced bananas on a plate in one layer. Cover with plastic wrap and freeze until completely firm. In a food processor or blender, combine frozen banana slices, ricotta cheese, and nutmeg. Purée until smooth. Divide into 4 dessert bowls. Top with strawberries or blueberries.

**Vegetarian. Serves 4.**

# Green-Grape Cream

This quick dessert is good enough to serve at an adult dinner party. For children under five, cut the grapes in half or quarters.

2 cups seedless green grapes
3/4 cup low-fat sour cream
1 tablespoon honey

In a small bowl, combine grapes, sour cream, and honey. Mix well. Chill and serve.

**Vegetarian. Serves 4.**

# Peanut Butter Cookies

Because peanut butter has a fairly high fat content, we make these cookies with a product called Lighter Bake; it's a fat-free, fruit-based replacement for butter and oil.

1/4 cup Lighter Bake (or 1/2 cup margarine)

1/2 cup peanut butter

1 1/4 cups all-purpose flour

1/2 cup honey or maple syrup

1 egg or equivalent Egg Replacer

1/2 teaspoon baking soda

1/2 teaspoon baking powder

1/2 teaspoon vanilla

Preheat oven to 375 degrees. In a large bowl, combine Lighter Bake and peanut butter. Beat on medium speed with an electric mixer for 30 seconds. Add 1/2 cup of the flour, then honey, egg, baking soda, baking powder, and vanilla. Beat until well combined. Beat in remaining flour. Shape dough into 1-inch balls. Place on ungreased cookie sheet. Flatten with a fork. Bake for 7–9 minutes, or until bottoms are lightly browned. Transfer to a wire rack to cool.

**Vegetarian. Makes 3 dozen.**

# Pumpkin Cookies

These cookies are sure kid pleasers for winter holidays—and all year-round.

4 tablespoons light margarine or Lighter Bake

1/4 cup maple syrup

1 tablespoon water

1 teaspoon vanilla

1 cup canned pumpkin

1 cup unbleached white flour

1/2 cup wheat germ

1/2 cup rolled oats

1 teaspoon baking soda

1 teaspoon cinnamon

1/2 teaspoon ginger

1/2 teaspoon nutmeg

1/4 teaspoon allspice

Preheat oven to 350 degrees. Spray a cookie sheet with vegetable cooking spray. In a large mixing bowl, combine margarine, maple syrup, water, and vanilla. With an electric mixer, beat on low speed until well blended. Add pumpkin and beat until thoroughly combined. In a separate bowl, combine flour, wheat germ, rolled oats, baking soda, cinnamon, ginger, nutmeg, and allspice. Mix thoroughly. Add to pumpkin mixture and stir until well blended. Drop batter by rounded teaspoons onto prepared cookie sheet. Bake 12–14 minutes. Remove to a wire rack to cool.

**Vegan. Makes 4 dozen.**

# Red, White & Blue Sundaes

This is a natural for a Fourth of July backyard party. For more fun, let the kids put the toppings on their own sundaes.

2 cups frozen strawberries, no sugar added

Pinch of ground nutmeg

1/4 cup maple syrup

4 cups low-fat vanilla frozen yogurt or
   frozen soy dessert

1 cup fresh blueberries

3/4 cup low-fat granola

In a food processor or blender, purée strawberries and nutmeg until smooth. While blender is going, slowly add maple syrup and blend well. Set sauce aside. Divide frozen yogurt evenly among four serving bowls. Top each with strawberry sauce, blueberries, and granola.

**Vegetarian. Serves 4.**

# Yogurt Pie Crust

Try this low-fat pie crust recipe with Puzzling Pumpkin Pie, page 97.

1/4 cup olive oil

1/2 cup plain low-fat yogurt

3/4 cup unbleached all-purpose flour

1/2 cup whole-wheat pastry flour

1/8 teaspoon salt

Preheat oven to 400 degrees. In a large bowl, combine the oil and yogurt, mixing well. In a separate bowl, combine the flours and salt. Stir into the oil and yogurt mixture, 1/4 cup at a time, until well combined. Roll the mixture into a ball and flatten it into a thick pancake. Wrap in waxed paper and refrigerate 20 minutes.

Between two sheets of waxed paper, roll the chilled dough into a large circle. Transfer dough into a 9- or 10-inch pie plate and chill for 15 minutes. Add pie filling of your choice and bake according to directions.

NOTE: To bake unfilled, preheat oven to 400 degrees. Prick crust on bottom and sides with a fork. Bake for 15 to 20 minutes or until golden brown. Cool before adding filling.

**Vegetarian. Makes one 10-inch pie
   crust.**

# Scrumptious Carrot Cake

Kids just seem to naturally love carrot cake. This particular cake freezes very well, keeping for up to three months, unfrosted. Frost the cake just before you're ready to serve it. We recommend our Cream Cheese Frosting.

3/4 cup walnuts

3–4 medium carrots, peeled and grated (about 1 1/2 cups)

3/4 cup unsweetened crushed pineapple, drained

3/4 cup oil

1/2 cup honey

1/2 cup molasses

4 egg whites

1 1/2 teaspoons vanilla

1 cup unbleached white flour

1/2 cup whole-wheat pastry flour

1 1/2 teaspoons cinnamon

1 1/2 teaspoons baking soda

1/8 teaspoon nutmeg

Preheat oven to 350 degrees. Spray the bottom of two 8-inch round cake pans with vegetable cooking spray. On a cookie sheet, toast walnuts 7–10 minutes, stirring occasionally. Let cool, then process in a food processor until finely ground.

In a large bowl, combine carrots, pineapple, and walnuts. Set aside. With electric mixer on medium-high, beat oil, honey, and molasses until thickened. Add egg whites, one at a time. Stir in vanilla. Sift dry ingredients three times. Add sifted ingredients and carrot mixture to honey mixture. Beat on low speed 3 minutes. Pour into pans. Bake 35–40 minutes or until tops of cakes spring back when touched lightly in the center. Cool on wire rack. Frost layers separately or stack for a 2-layer cake.

**Vegetarian. Serves 12.**

# Cream Cheese Frosting

The perfect companion to any carrot cake. The tofu cuts down on the amount of cream cheese needed.

4 ounces tofu, soft

3 ounces low-fat cream cheese (Neufchâtel), softened

2 tablespoons honey

1/4 teaspoon vanilla

Baby carrots, optional

In a small bowl, blend ingredients with an electric mixer at high speed until smooth and creamy. For a festive look, edge cake with tiny, baby carrots, sliced once lengthwise.

**Vegetarian. Frosts one Scrumptious Carrot Cake.**

## Baked Apples

Mom made 'em. Grandma made 'em. This classic treat never goes out of style.

4 large apples

1/2 cup water

1/2 cup apple juice

1/2 cup raisins

1/2 cup slivered almonds

Dash cinnamon

Preheat oven to 350 degrees. Core whole apples and peel off skin around top. Place in baking dish. In a small bowl, combine water, apple juice, raisins, and almonds. Place even amounts in cavity of each apple. Sprinkle with cinnamon. Bake 30–50 minutes until tender. Baste during baking with cooking juices. Cool slightly.

**Vegan. Serves 4.**

## Banana Bread

Here's a recipe that proves you can bake wonderful things without using eggs or refined sugar. Slice it, toast it, and serve with 100 percent fruit jelly, or just by itself.

1 1/2 cups whole-wheat flour

1/4 cup wheat germ

1 teaspoon cinnamon

2 teaspoons baking powder

1/2 teaspoon baking soda

1/4 teaspoon salt

1/4 teaspoon nutmeg

1/2 cup walnuts, chopped (optional)

1/4 cup unsweetened applesauce

1/2 cup maple syrup

1/8 teaspoon vanilla

1 cup extra ripe banana, mashed

1 tablespoon water

Preheat oven to 350 degrees. In a small bowl, combine dry ingredients, including walnuts. In a separate bowl, combine remaining ingredients and stir into dry mixture until thoroughly combined. The batter will be thick. Spread in an 8 1/2 x 4–inch loaf pan sprayed with vegetable cooking spray. Bake 35–40 minutes or until a toothpick inserted in middle comes out clean. Cool for 10 minutes. Transfer from pan to a cooling rack and cool completely before cutting.

**Vegan. Serves 8.**

**Better than** peanut butter & jelly

# Toddler
## recipes

Toddlers can drive you wild with their strange, repetitive food demands. Marty's grandson Joey has eaten only "Chicken" Tenders for dinner for two years now and shows no signs of tiring of them! Sometimes toddlers don't eat at all, and then we worry about malnourishment. One of the keys to success with feeding toddlers is, first, start them young—right at the high-chair stage—with mashed food from the family table, and give them a wide variety of foods so they get used to lots of different tastes. Second, you can be creative with how you mix their favorite foods and sometimes include highly nutritious ingredients in the dish. And, last, try to keep refined sugar and salt out of your toddler's diet and feed her only natural-sugar foods such as fresh fruit.

Toddlers don't need a lot of food. For example, at ages 1 to 2 years, the typical toddler portion is about 1/4 to 1/2 of an adult-sized portion. You might do better if you offer small amounts of food rather than try to feed your toddler a large meal all at once. Plus, give your toddler choices. As an example, offer two items and let her choose. That way you still have a say in what she eats. Patience is a virtue when it comes to toddler eating habits! Above all, don't let food and mealtimes become a confrontation and battle of wills.

# Macaroni & Cheese

We sometimes add peas or broccoli to this casserole.

1/2 pound pasta (use a fun shape)

8 ounces cheddar cheese, shredded

4 ounces low-fat, plain yogurt

4 ounces of your child's favorite frozen vegetable

1/2 cup fresh whole-wheat bread crumbs (or wheat germ)

Preheat oven to 350 degrees. Cook macaroni according to package directions; drain well. Transfer noodles to a medium-sized bowl and mix in cheese, yogurt, and vegetable; blend well. Pour into medium casserole dish and top with bread crumbs or wheat germ. Bake for 20 minutes.

**Vegetarian. Serves 3.**

# Macaroni & Cheese II

A second healthy variation on the traditional dish.

3/4 pound fresh broccoli, chopped

1 pound penne or tube pasta

Dash salt and pepper

3/4 cup low-fat ricotta cheese

3/4 cup low-fat mozzarella cheese, very thinly sliced

3/4 cup Romano cheese, grated

1 egg, beaten

1/4 cup wheat germ

1/8 cup sunflower seeds

Preheat oven to 425 degrees. Bring a large pot of water to boil; add broccoli and cook until bright green and still very crisp. Remove with a slotted spoon and set aside. Add pasta and cook until just done. Drain.

Spray a 9 x 13–inch baking pan with vegetable cooking spray. Arrange a layer of pasta on bottom of pan. Add layer of broccoli, then ricotta. Place mozzarella on top. Sprinkle with grated cheese. Repeat layers and end with a layer of pasta on top. Top with beaten egg. Sprinkle on wheat germ and sunflower seeds. Bake for 20 minutes.

**Vegetarian. Serves 6.**

## Dinosaur "Chicken" Tenders

This is so much better than the packaged, frozen, real chicken tenders, which are full of salt and sugar.

1 package chicken substitute
Wheat germ

Preheat oven to 350 degrees. With a dinosaur-shaped cookie cutter, cut meatless chicken pieces. Roll in wheat germ until thoroughly coated. Place in a baking pan sprayed with vegetable cooking spray. Cook for 15–20 minutes until golden brown. If necessary, run under broiler at the end to finish browning. Serve with Firefighter "French Fries," page 46, and Joey & Michael's "Trees," page 108.

**Vegetarian. Serves 3**

## Egghead

Create faces just like the game Mr. Potato Head. Be creative and add some additional veggies, nuts, or seeds.

2 eggs, hard-boiled, cut in half lengthwise
Roasted pumpkin seeds, unsalted
Small slice red pepper
A few cooked whole-wheat noodles

Using the above ingredients, create faces with your toddler.

**Vegetarian. Serves 1–2.**

## Michael's Fabulous Peanut Butter Sandwich

Marty's toddler grandson actually made up this sandwich and loves it to this day. This sandwich will provide lots of protein.

2 slices whole-wheat or multigrain bread with crusts cut off
1 tablespoon peanut butter
1/2 apple, cut in thin slices
1 slice cheddar cheese or your toddler's favorite cheese

Smooth peanut butter on one slice. Top with apple slices and cheese. Put other piece of bread on top and cut into four squares.

**Vegetarian. Serves 2–4.**

# Fruit Spritzer

This is a great and healthy substitute for soda.

4 cups sugar-free cranberry juice

4 cups seltzer water

1 orange, seeded and thinly sliced

Combine juice and seltzer water in large pitcher. Add orange slices and chill well.

**Vegan. Serves 8.**

# <Your Child's Name> Mini-Meatless Loaf

(e.g., Joey's Mini-Meatless Loaf)

Your child will look forward to his very own entrée and perhaps this will be the beginning of a love of cooking.

1 fresh veggie burger, crumbled

Wheat germ

Celery, very finely chopped

1 tablespoon catsup

1 teaspoon cheddar or mozzarella cheese, shredded

Mix all ingredients well. Add wheat germ, if necessary, until you get a consistency that holds together. Form into a patty and broil or cook in a fry pan coated with vegetable oil.

**Vegetarian. Serves 1–2.**

# Orangeade

This is much better than boxed fruit juices and a lot more fun for your toddler.

1 large can (16 ounces) frozen orange juice concentrate

4 oranges

8 cups seltzer water

4 cups water

Thaw juice concentrate. Cut oranges in thin slices and remove seeds. Mix juice concentrate, seltzer, and water in a large pitcher. Add orange slices. Stir and chill well.

**Vegan. Serves 12.**

# Joey & Michael's "Trees"

Marty used "Trees" to intrigue and entice the twins when they were young toddlers. They still call broccoli "trees"!

1/2 pound fresh broccoli, separated into small florets with short stalks

A few broccoli stalks, sliced very thinly then cut into small sticks to look like grass

Mashed potatoes (optional)

In a steamer or small saucepan, steam broccoli florets until just done or about 3–5 minutes. Place on plate with "grass." Be creative and use mashed potatoes as "clouds."

**Vegan. Serves 2**

## English Muffin Pizzas

Vary the toppings depending on your child's creativity or what's in your refrigerator. Use broccoli, tomatoes, or thinly sliced zucchini—or try sunflower seeds or soy nuts.

4 whole-wheat English muffins, sliced in halves

1 can (6 ounces) tomato paste

8 slices mozzarella cheese

Preheat oven to 350 degrees. Spread tomato paste evenly over each English muffin half. Top each with a cheese slice. Bake 10–15 minutes until cheese is melted.

**Vegetarian. Serves 8.**

## Sandwich Stars

Here's a neat way to reward your child's good behavior with a star.

8 slices whole-grain bread, crusts removed

Baba Ghanouj, page 47

bean sprouts

1 cup of each, chopped: cucumbers, radishes, tomatoes

Using a large star-shaped cookie cutter, cut each piece of bread into a star shape. Spread equal amounts of Baba Ghanouj on each star. Top with equal amounts of chopped veggies and then a nebula of bean sprouts.

**Vegan. Serves 8.**

## Potted Muffins

You can buy "muffin-sized" clay flowerpots for this recipe at any garden or hardware store. After the muffins have been eaten, rinse the pots and fill with potting soil. Give the kids a choice of seeds to plant. Beans, lettuce, tomato, squash, carrot, corn, and sunflowers are good choices.

2 cups multigrain pancake and waffle mix

1 cup fresh orange, chopped

1/4 cup vegetable oil

1/4 cup honey

3/4 cup water

Preheat oven to 400 degrees. In a medium bowl stir all ingredients until just smooth. Line 12 brand-new, washed and well-oiled, clay mini-flowerpots with cupcake liners, and spoon-in batter. Bake for 20–25 minutes or until tops of muffins spring back when touched. Cool in pots.

**Vegetarian. Makes 12 muffins.**

## Rice Pudding

A great dessert for little ones.

1 cup cooked brown rice

2/3 cup raisins

2 ripe bananas, peeled and mashed

1/2 cup orange juice

1 teaspoon ground cinnamon

1/4 teaspoon ground nutmeg

Preheat oven to 350 degrees. In a food processor or blender combine all ingredients. Blend for 1 minute. Pour into a loaf pan sprayed with vegetable cooking spray. Bake for 20 minutes.

**Vegan. Serves 6.**


## Peanut Butter Kisses

These no-bake, high-energy snacks are guaranteed to disappear fast!

1 cup nonfat dry milk powder

1/2 cup natural peanut butter

1/4 cup honey

1/2 cup crispy rice cereal

Mix all ingredients together. Roll into balls. Refrigerate for 1 hour.

**Vegetarian. Makes 24 pieces.**


## Tea Biscuits

To the British, a biscuit is a kind of cookie. These "tea biscuits" are actually more like the American version, a kind of quick bread, tender and flaky.

1 3/4 cups unbleached flour

1/4 cup whole-wheat flour

1 tablespoon baking powder

1/4 teaspoon salt

4 tablespoons margarine

2 tablespoons low-fat cream cheese (Neufchâtel)

1 large egg, beaten, or equivalent Egg Replacer

3/4 cup soy or rice milk

Preheat oven to 375 degrees. In a large bowl combine the flours, baking powder, and salt, and mix well. Cut the margarine and cream cheese into the flour mixture until coarse crumbs are formed. Slowly add soy milk and egg or equivalent, constantly stirring, until dough forms into a tidy ball. Let dough sit for about 1 minute. On a slightly floured surface, knead dough 6–8 times, then pat it out until it's about 1/2-inch thick. With a glass or cup, cut biscuits out and place them, edges just touching, on an ungreased cookie sheet. Hold in refrigerator for at least 20 minutes but no more than 4 hours. Bake 20–25 minutes until slightly golden. Serve slightly warm with natural fruit jelly, if desired.

**Vegetarian. Makes 12 biscuits.**

# family
# **Menu** ideas

Here are a few suggestions for combinations of easy-to-make dishes that will satisfy the whole family.

**Sunday Brunch**

Fruity Juice, page 26

Tofu Scramble, page 27

Meatless breakfast links

Banana Pancakes, page 30

Berry Breakfast Parfait, page 29

**Sunday Dinner**

Portabella Mushroom "Steak" Dinner, page 85

Whole-grain linguini noodles

Cool Cucumber Salad, page 39

Stuffed Tomatoes, page 48

Fresh greens with oil and vinegar dressing

Green-Grape Cream, page 100

**Monday Morning Scramble!**

Fruity Juice, page 26

Apple-Carrot Muffins (made over the weekend and frozen), page 32

Make-Your-Own Granola, page 29

Sliced bananas

**Lunch at Home**

1. Carrot Salad Pita, page 59
   Polka-Dot Pea Soup, page 35
   Slices of unpeeled apple
   Chilled soy or rice milk

2. The Vegetarian Club, page 60
   Electrifying Fruit Salad, page 44
   Raw, diced vegetables
   Baba Ghanouj (for dipping), page 47

**Let-the-Kids-Make-Lunch Day**

Lettuce Wraps, page 62

Fabulous Fruit Salad, page 42

Whole-grain bread

Tomato soup (a low-fat and low-sodium brand)

**Weeknight Winner**

Beans & "Franks," page 79

Leftover, reheated brown rice

Orange & Green Salad, page 39

Red, White & Blue Sundaes, page 102

**Company for Dinner**

Creamy Broccoli Soup, page 34

Veggie Kabobs, page 80

Whole-wheat couscous

Whole-wheat French bread

Scrumptious Carrot Cake with Cream Cheese Frosting, page 103

**Fall Festival Dinner**

Stuffed Zucchini, page 84

Bulgur wheat

Organic greens salad

Blueberry & Yogurt Crunch, page 96

**Take a Mediterranean Cruise Tuesday**

Mediterranean "Chicken," page 73

Couscous

Broccoli with Sesame Seeds, page 52

Stewed carrots, onions, and tomatoes

Dates, figs, and prunes with yogurt

**Go Greek**

Greek Spaghetti, page 72

Fresh green beans

Baba Ghanouj, page 47

Greek bread

**Saturday Supper**

1. Veggie Burgers, page 63
   Firefighter "French Fries," page 46
   Nutty Beans, page 48
   Fresh greens salad
   Fabulous Fruit Salad, page 42

2. Zucchini Pizza, page 86
   Cartwheel Carrots, page 50
   Fresh spinach leaves with sliced cucumbers and tomatoes
   Apple Crumble, page 99

**Southwestern Party Buffet**

Taco Soup, page 34

Black Bean Chili, page 35

Corn Bread from Emily, page 49

Southwestern Pasta Casserole, page 66

Taco-less Taco Salad, page 76

Veggie Burritos, page 69

Natural, low-fat corn chips

Salsa

**Toddlers Make Their Own Dinner**

Michael's Fabulous Peanut Butter Sandwich, page 107
*A toddler creation!*

Egghead, page 107

Orangeade, page 108
*Let your little one pour the "fizzy" water then drop in the orange slices.*

Watermelon "Stars"
*Use a small star-shaped cookie cutter to cut out seedless watermelon slices.*

# Nutrition values
## of key ingredients

| Ingredient | Portion | Calories | Protein (Grams) | Fat (Grams) | Carbohydrates (Grams) |
|---|---|---|---|---|---|
| Apple, peeled | 1 medium | 72 | 0 | 0.4 | 19.0 |
| Applesauce, unsweetened | 1/2 cup | 53 | 0.2 | 0.1 | 13.8 |
| Banana | 1 medium | 105 | 1.2 | 0.6 | 26.7 |
| Beans, baked, vegetarian | 1 cup | 235 | 12.2 | 1.1 | 52.1 |
| Beans, black, cooked | 1 cup | 227 | 15.2 | 0.9 | 40.8 |
| Beans, green, cooked | 1/2 cup | 22 | 1.2 | 0.2 | 4.9 |
| Beans, kidney, cooked | 1 cup | 216 | 13.4 | 0.9 | 39.9 |
| Beans, navy, canned | 1 cup | 296 | 19.7 | 1.1 | 53.6 |
| Blackberries, raw | 1/2 cup | 37 | 0.5 | 0.3 | 9.2 |
| Blueberries | 1 cup | 82 | 1.0 | 0.6 | 20.5 |
| Bread, cracked wheat | 1 slice | 66 | 2.3 | 0.9 | 12.5 |
| Bread, pita | 1 piece | 106 | 4.0 | 0.6 | 20.6 |
| Bread, whole-wheat | 1 slice | 61 | 2.4 | 1.1 | 11.4 |
| Broccoli, cooked | 1/2 cup | 23 | 2.0 | 0.3 | 4.0 |
| Buckwheat groats, cooked | 1 cup | 182 | 8.0 | 1.2 | 39.5 |
| Bulgur, cooked | 1 cup | 152 | 5.6 | 0.4 | 33.8 |
| Canola oil | 1 Tbs | 124 | 0 | 14.0 | 0 |
| Cantaloupe, raw | 1 cup pieces | 57 | 1.4 | 0.4 | 13.4 |
| Carob | 3 oz bar | 453 | 28.0 | 10.9 | 41.9 |
| Carrot, raw | 1 medium | 31 | 0.7 | 0.1 | 7.3 |
| Cheese, cream, light | 1 oz | 62 | 2.9 | 1.8 | 4.7 |
| Cheese, feta | 1 oz | 75 | 4.0 | 6.0 | 1.2 |
| Cheese, mozzarella, part-skim | 1 oz | 72 | 6.9 | 4.5 | 0.8 |
| Cheese, Parmesan, grated | 1 Tbs | 23 | 2.1 | 1.5 | 0.2 |
| Cheese, ricotta, part-skim | 1/2 cup | 171 | 14.1 | 9.8 | 6.4 |
| Chickpeas, canned | 1 cup | 200 | 10.0 | 4.0 | 32.0 |
| Chocolate, baking, unsweetened | 1 oz | 148 | 2.9 | 15.7 | 8.0 |
| Cocoa, unsweetened | 1/3 cup, 1 oz | 115 | 7.6 | 3.6 | 12.7 |

| Ingredient | Portion | Calories | Protein (Grams) | Fat (Grams) | Carbohydrates (Grams) |
|---|---|---|---|---|---|
| Corn, canned | 1/2 cup | 66 | 2.2 | 0.8 | 15.2 |
| Couscous, cooked | 1 cup | 201 | 6.8 | 0.3 | 41.6 |
| Cucumber, sliced | 1/2 cup | 7 | 0.3 | 0.1 | 1.5 |
| Dates, dried | 10 | 228 | 1.6 | 0.4 | 61.0 |
| Dates, dried, chopped | 1/4 cup | 130 | 1.0 | 0 | 31.0 |
| Egg Replacer | 1 1/2 tsp, dry | 14 | 0 | 0 | 3.3 |
| Egg | 1 boiled | 77 | 6.3 | 5.3 | 0.6 |
| Eggplant, raw | 1/2 cup | 11 | 0.5 | 0 | 2.6 |
| Flour, all-purpose enriched | 1 cup | 455 | 12.9 | 1.2 | 95.4 |
| Flour, whole-wheat | 1 cup | 407 | 16.4 | 2.2 | 87.1 |
| Granola, Post | 1/4 cup or 1 oz | 128 | 2.4 | 4.1 | 20.7 |
| Grapefruit, raw, white | 1/2 medium | 37 | 0.7 | 0.1 | 9.5 |
| Grapes | 1 cup | 58 | 0.6 | 0.3 | 15.8 |
| Honey, raw | 1 Tbs | 64 | 0.1 | 0 | 17.3 |
| Hummus | 1 cup | 420 | 12.1 | 20.8 | 49.6 |
| Juice, cranberry | 6 oz | 108 | 0 | 0.1 | 27.4 |
| Juice, orange | 6 oz | 87 | 0 | 0 | 22.0 |
| Kiwifruit, peeled | 1 medium | 46 | 0.8 | 0.3 | 11.3 |
| Leeks, raw | 1/4 cup chopped | 16 | 0.4 | 0.1 | 3.7 |
| Lemon, raw | 1 medium | 17 | 0.6 | 0.2 | 5.4 |
| Lettuce, romaine, raw, shredded | 1/2 cup | 4 | 0.5 | 0.1 | 0.7 |
| Macaroni, enriched, cooked | 1 cup | 197 | 6.7 | 0.9 | 39.7 |
| Mango, peeled | 1 medium | 135 | 1.1 | 0.6 | 35.2 |
| Maple syrup | 1 Tbs | 52 | 0 | 0 | 13.4 |
| Mayonnaise, soy | 1 Tbs | 99 | 0.2 | 11.0 | 0.4 |
| Meat substitute, Harvest Burgers for Recipes | 2/3 cup | 90 | 14.0 | 0 | 8.0 |
| Milk, cow's whole, 3.3% fat | 1 cup | 150 | 8.0 | 8.2 | 11.4 |
| Milk, cow's skim | 1 cup | 86 | 8.4 | 0.4 | 11.9 |
| Milk, soy, plain, not reduced fat | 1 cup | 79 | 6.6 | 4.6 | 4.3 |

| Ingredient | Portion | Calories | Protein (Grams) | Fat (Grams) | Carbohydrates (Grams) |
|---|---|---|---|---|---|
| Molasses | 1 Tbs | 53 | 0 | 0 | 13.8 |
| Mushrooms, raw, pieces | 1/2 cup | 9 | 0.7 | 0.2 | 1.6 |
| Oatmeal, cooked | 1 cup | 145 | 6.0 | 2.4 | 25.2 |
| Okra, boiled | 1/2 cup slices | 25 | 1.5 | 0.1 | 5.8 |
| Olive oil | 1 Tbs | 119 | 0 | 13.5 | 0 |
| Onion, raw, chopped | 1/2 cup | 30 | 0.9 | 0.1 | 6.9 |
| Orange, Mandarin, canned, unsweetened | 1/2 cup | 46 | 0.8 | 0 | 11.9 |
| Orange, peeled | 1 medium | 65 | 1.4 | 0.1 | 16.3 |
| Peach | 1 medium | 37 | 0.6 | 0.1 | 9.7 |
| Peanut butter | 2 Tbs | 188 | 7.9 | 16.0 | 6.6 |
| Peanuts, dry roasted | 1 oz | 164 | 6.6 | 13.9 | 6.0 |
| Pear, raw | 1 medium | 98 | 0.7 | 0.7 | 25.1 |
| Peas, green, cooked | 1/2 cup | 67 | 4.3 | 0.2 | 12.5 |
| Pepper, sweet, raw, chopped | 1/2 cup | 13 | 0.4 | 0.1 | 3.2 |
| Pineapple, canned in juice | 1 cup | 150 | 1.0 | 0.2 | 39.2 |
| Pineapple, raw | 1 cup pieces | 77 | 0.6 | 0.7 | 19.2 |
| Plantain, cooked | 1 cup slices | 179 | 2.0 | 0.3 | 48.0 |
| Popcorn, plain, popped | 3 1/2 cups | 108 | 3.4 | 1.2 | 22.1 |
| Potato, sweet, without skin, baked | 1 | 118 | 2.0 | 0.1 | 27.7 |
| Potato, without skin, baked | 1 | 145 | 3.1 | 0.2 | 33.6 |
| Pound cake, Pepperidge Farm | 1.1 oz | 131 | 1.5 | 7.0 | 15.5 |
| Pumpkin, canned | 1/2 cup | 41 | 1.3 | 0.3 | 9.9 |
| Quinoa grain, cooked | 1/2 cup | 318 | 11.1 | 4.9 | 58.6 |
| Raisins | 2/3 cup | 300 | 3.2 | 0.5 | 79.1 |
| Rice, brown long grain, cooked | 1 cup | 216 | 5.0 | 1.8 | 44.8 |
| Rice, white Minute, cooked | 2/3 cup | 120 | 3.0 | 0 | 27.0 |
| Rice, wild, cooked | 1 cup | 166 | 6.5 | 0.6 | 35.0 |
| Safflower oil | 1 Tbs | 120 | 0 | 13.6 | 0 |
| Sour cream, light | 1 Tbs | 20 | 1.0 | 2.0 | 1.0 |
| Spaghetti, cooked | 1 cup | 197 | 6.7 | 0.9 | 39.7 |

| Ingredient | Portion | Calories | Protein (Grams) | Fat (Grams) | Carbohydrates (Grams) |
|---|---|---|---|---|---|
| Spaghetti, whole-wheat, cooked | 1 cup | 174 | 7.5 | 0.8 | 37.2 |
| Spinach, frozen, cooked | 1/2 cup | 27 | 3 | 0.2 | 5.1 |
| Squash, spaghetti, baked | 1 cup | 23 | 0.5 | 0.2 | 5.0 |
| Strawberries, raw | 1 cup | 45 | 0.9 | 0.6 | 10.5 |
| Sunflower seeds | 1 oz | 162 | 6.5 | 14.1 | 5.5 |
| Tofu, raw, regular | 1/2 cup | 94 | 10.0 | 5.9 | 2.3 |
| Tomato, raw | 1 medium | 26 | 1.0 | 0.4 | 5.7 |
| Tomato, stewed, canned | 1/2 cup | 34 | 1.2 | 0.2 | 8.3 |
| Tortilla, enriched | 1 | 67 | 2.1 | 1.1 | 12.8 |
| Walnuts, English, raw | 1 oz | 180 | 4.0 | 18.0 | 5.0 |
| Wheat Chex | 2/3 cup or 1 oz | 100 | 2.9 | 0.7 | 23.0 |
| Wheat germ | 1/4 cup | 104 | 6.7 | 2.8 | 15.0 |
| Yogurt, frozen, soft serve | 1/2 cup | 114 | 2.8 | 4.0 | 17.4 |
| Zucchini, raw | 1/2 cup | 9 | 0.8 | 0.1 | 1.9 |

**Better than** peanut butter & jelly

# Resources for vegetarians

## National Organizations & Sources of Information

**American Dietetic Association**
120 South Riverside Plaza, Suite 2000
Chicago, Il 60606-6995
800-877-1600
www.eatright.org

**The American Vegan Society**
P.O. Box 369
Malaga, NJ 08328
856-694-2887
Fax: 856-694-2288
www.americanvegan.org/

**The North American Vegetarian Society**
P.O. Box 72
Dolgeville, NY 13329
518-568-7970
www.navs-online.org

**People for the Ethical Treatment of Animals**
501 Front Street
Norfolk, VA 23510
757-622-PETA (7382)
Fax: 757-628-0782
e-mail: info@peta-on-line.org
www.peta-online.org

**Vegetarian Awareness Network**
800-USA-VEGE (24-hour message)

**The Vegetarian Resource Group**
P.O. Box 1463
Baltimore, MD 21203
410-366-8343
e-mail: vrg@vrg.org
www.vrg.org/

**Vegetarian Union of North America**
P.O. Box 9710
Washington, DC 20016
e-mail: vuna@ivu.org
www.ivu.org/vuna/english.html

# Vegetarian Publications

## Magazines

### Vegetarian Gourmet
P.O. Box 7641
Riverton, NJ 08077
Vegetarian Journal
P.O. Box 1463
Baltimore MD 21203
410-366-VEGE
www.vrg.org/journal/

### Vegetarian Times
300 N. Continental Blvd., Suite 650
El Segundo, CA 90245
310-356-4100
800-435-9610
Fax: 310-356-4110
www.vegetariantimes.com

### Vegetarian Voice
P.O. Box 72
Dolgeville, NY 13329
518-568-7970
(Published by The North American
  Vegetarian Society)
www.navs-online.org

### Veggie Life
P.O. Box 57159
Boulder, CO 80322
e-mail: support@veggielife.com

www.veggielife.com

## Newsletters

### Ahimsa
American Vegan Society
P.O. Box H
Malaga, NJ 08328
609-694-2887
www.americanvegan.org

### VUNA Views
P.O. Box 9710
Washington, DC 20016
www.ivu.org/vuna/news/

# Mail Order Companies

**Apple Valley Market**
9067 US 31
Berrien Springs, MI 49103
800-237-7436
www.avnf.com
*Meat substitutes, nuts, seeds, soy cheese*

**Body Ecology Products**
218 Laredo Drive, Suite A
Decatur, GA 30030
800-511-2660
Fax: 404-378-3866
*Kefir products*

**Dixie's Diner Club**
P.O. Box 1969
Tomball, TX 77377
800-233-3668 for catalog
www.dixiediner.com
*TVP (textured vegetable protein) prod-
  ucts, condiments, and kitchen gadgets*

**ENER-G Foods, Inc.**
P.O. Box 84487
Seattle, WA 98124-5787
800-331-5222
www.ener-g.com
*Egg Replacer and other products*

**Garden Spot Distributors**
438 White Oak Road
Route 1, Box 729A
New Holland, PA 17557
800-829-5100
www.gardenspotdist.com
*Bulk foods and specialty items*

**Better than** peanut butter & jelly

**The Mail Order Catalog for Healthy Eating**
P.O. Box 180
Summertown, TN 38483
800-695-2241
www.healthy-eating.com
*Meat substitutes, soy products, books*

**Mountain Ark Natural Foods**
146 Londonderry Turnpike, Unit 10
Hooksett, NH 03106
888-392-9237
e-mail: masupport@mountainark.com
www.mountainark.com/
*All vegetarian natural products*

**Natural Way Mills, Inc.**
24509 390th St. NE
Middle River, MN 56737
218-222-3677
www.naturalwaymills.com
*Organic whole-grains and flours*

**Organic Provisions**
Box 756
Richboro, PA 18954-0756
800-490-0044
www.orgfood.com
*Organic natural foods*

**Walnut Acres**
The Hain Celestial Group
4600 Sleepytime Drive
Boulder, CO 80301
www.walnutacres.com
*Organic vegetarian foods*

**Walton Feed**
135 North 10th
P.O. Box 397
Montpelier, ID 83254
800-269-8563
www.waltonfeed.com
*Dehydrated and dry vegetables, beans, grains, and flours; organic selection*

**The Whole Earth Vegetarian Catalog**
Lumen Foods
409 Scott Street
Lake Charles, LA 70601
800-256-2253
www.soybean.com
*Meat substitutes, soy products*

**Whole Foods Market**
550 Bowie Street
Austin, TX 78703
www.wholefoodsmarket.com (product orders are through www.gaiam.com)
*Meals and sides, snacks, beverages, and cooking essentials*

# Online Services/Internet

**Loma Linda University**
www.llu.edu/llu/nutrition/fabfacts.html
*Vegetarian shopping list, shopping tips, substitutions, and recipes*

**Nutrispeak: Vesanto Melina RD**
www.nutrispeak.com/foodguides.htm
*Vegan and vegetarian food pyramids based on the US Food Guide. The Vegan Rainbow and the Vegetarian Rainbow based on the Canadian Food Guide*

**Recipes around the World**
International Vegetarian Union (IVU)
www.ivu.org/recipes/
*Almost 1,800 vegan recipes in a searchable database*

**The Road to Vegetarianism**
Vegetarians in Paradise
www.vegparadise.com
*Information on alternative foods for vegetarians, including meat, dairy, and egg alternatives*

## Vegetarian Glossary

**Vegetarian Times**
www.vegetariantimes.com/resources/
glossary/asp
*Definitions of foods often eaten by
vegetarians*

## Listservs

**SCI-Veg**
www.waste.org/sci-veg

**Veg-News**
Veg-news@enviroolink.com

## Vegetarian Web Pages

**Vegetarian Resource Group**
www.veg.org/veg/

**Vegetarian Youth Network**
www.geocities.com/RainForest/Vines/4482/

**World Guide to Vegetarianism**
www.vegweb.com/

## Recommended Books

*Becoming Vegan: The Complete Guide to
Adopting a Healthy Plant-based Diet.*
Brenda Davis, RD and Vesanto Melina,
MS, RD. Book Publishing Company,
2000.

*The Complete Book of Food.* Carol Ann
Rinzler. World Almanac, 1987.

*Diet for a Small Planet, 20th Anniversary
Edition.* Frances Moore Lappe. Ballantine
Books, 1991.

*Dr. Charles Attwood's Low-Fat Prescription for
Kids: A Pediatrician's Program of Preventive
Nutrition.* Charles Attwood, MD. Viking-
Penguin, 1995.

*Food Values of Portions Commonly Used.* Jean
A.T. Pennington. J.B. Lippincott Company,
1994.

*Good Food Today, Great Kids Tomorrow.* Jay
Gordon with Antonia Barnes Boyle. Michael
Wiese Productions, 1994.

*Honest Pretzels: And 64 Other Amazing Recipes
for Cooks Ages 8 & Up.* Mollie Katzen.
Tricycle Press, 1999.

*New Vegetarian Baby.* Sharon K. Yntema and
Christine H. Beard. McBooks Press, 2000.

*Pretend Soup and Other Real Recipes: A
Cookbook for Preschoolers & Up.* Mollie
Katzen and Ann Henderson. Tricycle Press,
1994.

*Salad People And More Real Recipes: A New
Cookbook for Preschoolers & Up.* Mollie
Katzen. Tricycle Press, 2005.

*Vegan: The New Ethics of Eating.* Erik Marcus.
McBooks Press, 1998.

*Vegan & Vegetarian FAQ: Answers to Your
Frequently Asked Questions.* Davida Gypsy
Breier; Nutrition Section by Reed Mangels,
PhD, RD. The Vegetarian Resource Group,
2001.

*The Vegetarian Way.* Virginia Messina, MPH,
RD and Mark Messina, PhD. Crown Trade
Paperbacks, 1996.

# Index

**Better than** peanut butter & jelly